A Caring Church

A Caring Church

THROUGH SHEPHERDING MINISTRIES

Charles A. Ver Straten

BAKER BOOK HOUSE

Grand Rapids, Michigan 49516

This book is a revision and expansion of an earlier title, *How to Start Lay-Shepherding Ministries*, © 1983.

The New International Version © 1978 by New York International Bible Society is used as the primary Scripture source in this book. Other translations used are the Revised Standard Version (RSV) and the King James Version (KJV). There is one reference to the Good News Bible.

To the deacons and deaconesses
who have shared the ministry
of pastoral care with me.

You have been my partners
in shepherding God's people.

This is your story.
I thank you and salute you.

Contents

Appendixes

Foreword

This book makes good sense. And well it should. Charles A. Ver Straten is a sheep rancher, a trained theologian, and a pastor. He is also a person totally dedicated to serving God through bringing new people into a personal relationship with Jesus Christ and into the fellowship of the local church. Put all of these qualities together and you come out with a practical formula for the growth of the church both in quantity and in quality.

In the first place it makes sense *biblically*. The body of Christ, the church, is an organism with Jesus as the head and every member of the body functioning with one or more spiritual gifts. God distributes these gifts throughout the body so that each Christian can minister to others. Christians who are not using their gifts are living a sub-biblical lifestyle. Too many churches today expect the ministry of the church to be done by the pastor, not by the people of God, so the church members are largely spectators. One of the gifts that God gives to some believers is the gift of pastor. When they use it, not only are they fulfilled as individuals, but the whole church receives the benefits. Chuck Ver Straten explains carefully how the bulk of the pastoral work of the church can and should be done by lay people. This is God's design.

Secondly, it makes sense *organizationally*. On the sheep

ranch it is obvious that the only way large numbers of
sheep can be adequately cared for is to break them down
into smaller bands of sheep, assigned to one shepherd. It
does not require a degree in organizational management
to recognize the wisdom of such structuring. Jethro advised Moses to do it back in the days of the Exodus. This
book lays out, step-by-step, how the local church can be
structured, so that every member can receive the pastoral
care needed when it is needed without trying, sometimes
unsuccessfully, to break into the schedule of a busy senior
pastor or overextended staff member.

The third way *A Caring Church: Through Shepherding
Ministries* makes sense is *pastorally*. Over the past decade
or two the phenomenon of pastoral burnout has become
almost an epidemic. Research has shown that a chief cause
of burnout has been the tendency of pastors falling into
the trap of not being able to say *no* to demands on their
time. No pastor wants to say *no* to a church member who
is hurting and who needs pastoral care. Chuck Ver Straten,
who does have a pastor's heart, explains how a pastor can
say *yes* to any and all who need help without entering the
burnout syndrome. How? By delegating the ministry of
pastoral care to gifted and trained church members who—
believe it or not—can often do a better job at it than the
senior pastor could!

In the fourth place, *A Caring Church* makes sense *evan-
gelistically*. True evangelism brings people to Christ and
also into the body of Christ. True evangelism results in
church growth. Unless the members of the body are mobilized to do the ministry of the church, the growth of the
church will be limited. At least 80 percent of USA churches
are under two hundred in attendance. One of the major
reasons for this is that the members of those churches
unwisely demand that their pastor do all the ministry of
the church. A pastor can do all the ministry, but only up
to the two hundred barrier. If new members are going to
be brought into the church and if it is to cross the two

hundred barrier, it is essential to develop lay-shepherding ministries.

I know of no other book that so thoroughly and so wisely sets forth a design for developing quality pastoral care throughout the local church. Following the advice of Dr. Ver Straten will enable hundreds of churches to get out of the doldrums, to reach out powerfully to hurting people in their communities, to introduce them to the Great Shepherd, and to bring them into a warm, loving, local church where they can grow to be all God wants them to be.

C. PETER WAGNER
Professor of Church Growth
Fuller Theological Seminary

Preface

The acceptance and response to this book as originally published by Baker Book House in 1983 under the title *How to Start Lay Shepherding Ministries* was a pleasant surprise to me.

Many other pastors were obviously facing the same stresses and struggles of ministry and caregiving that had pressed my life to the wall. And the problem is as old as leadership with a concerned eye for the well-being of those being led has existed. Moses of old under the wise counsel of his father-in-law, Jethro, learned the lesson that I had relearned. The apostles themselves in Acts 6:2–4 rediscovered and applied the principle of shared ministry in the forming of the earliest Christian community.

So the Twelve gathered all the disciples together and said, "It would not be right for us to neglect the ministry of the word of God in order to wait on tables. Brothers, choose seven men from among you who are known to be full of the Spirit and wisdom. We will turn this responsibility over to them and give our attention to prayer and the ministry of the word" (Acts 6:2–4).

The multiplication and growth of larger local churches plus the advent of megasized congregations in the USA

13

and around the world has necessitated relearning this principle of shared shepherding ministries in every setting where solo pastoral care is not adequate.

Discipling was the buzz word, the theme and thrust of the seventies. *Shepherding* has become a predominant emphasis of the eighties.

Since publication of *How to Start Lay Shepherding Ministries* much material has been written. Cell ministries and group care with innovative approaches have proliferated. Much remains to be discovered about extending pastoral care through numerous styles of shepherding ministries.

Experience of new aspects has reinforced my conviction that trained laity produces strong, healthy, and vibrant churches.

After twelve years of pastoral leadership in the Denver area, I resigned to accept a call to pastor a church in the Northwest. The trained lay leaders shepherded the Mission Hills Church in a continuing growth pattern for a year's duration without the headship of a senior pastor. A wise, new senior pastor has bridged our ministries and is leading a larger flock to greater things.

The new challenge, Emmanuel Baptist Church of Mount Vernon, Washington, greatly benefited from the development and training of laity to a shepherding ministry and becoming a shared pastoral leadership.

That church was one of the strongest evangelical influences between Seattle and Vancouver, Canada, until a major church division left its remaining members emotionally wounded and directionless. An identity crisis followed with the repeated question, "Who are we anymore?"

I saw lay shepherds care, minister, and heal. They discovered Christ's purpose for that church and its reason for being. Healing happened, and a whole church came to health. This story needs to be added to the original saga. These scriptural principles apply and work anywhere in every situation.

The subject of this book with its additions is as pertinent today as it was in its original edition.

Today, the Good Shepherd from his throne room, surveying people in communities the world over, expresses the same heart concern described in Matthew 9:36, 37:

When he saw the crowds, he had compassion on them, because they were harassed and helpless, like sheep without a shepherd. Then he said to his disciples, "The harvest is plentiful but the workers are few."

Trained shepherds, clergy, and laity, gifted for the pastoral ministry by his spirit will continue:

. . . to prepare God's people for works of service, so that the body of Christ may be built up until we all reach unity in the faith and in the knowledge of the Son of God and become mature, attaining to the whole measure of the fullness of Christ (Eph. 4:12, 13).

I am deeply indebted to the lay people who have been partners with me in shepherding ministries. I have learned from them in their on-the-job-training experiences. I am continuing to learn that I am part of a team.

Peter Wagner has been a personal inspiration since the days we sat together in alphabetized order in classes at Fuller Theological Seminary. His recommendation of this book in its original edition as an answer for solving the need for quality pastoral care in growing larger churches made him the appropriate choice for writing the foreword to this book. I appreciate his encouragement and his words.

Naomi Tuttle, an indispensable member of one of our present shepherding teams, has enthusiastically and competently supplied the secretarial skills for the manuscript of this revision. I commend her for her invaluable contribution.

Always I am reminded that I am one member of a winning team that is empowered by his Spirit. The credit is always to him.

CHARLES A. VER STRATEN
Bethel Baptist Church
Greeley, Colorado

Introduction

An unrealistic expectation of the ministry and the role of the senior pastor exists in church life today. Many streams flow into and fill this reservoir of expectation.

Today's church milieu has a growing number of super-churches led by unusually gifted pastors who from all appearance function like superstars. Many congregations measure their own ministers by the perceived standard set by these famous ministers.

The average pastor has accumulated interior driving expectations of himself and his own ministry that do not match his talents or giftedness.

Perhaps the treadmill started in seminary and continued upward from that time. It was there he unconsciously absorbed attitudes of professors and fellow seminarians that formed an image of what an "ideal" minister ought to be. Somewhere in the process he forgot his own uniqueness, the special spiritual gift-mix that God has given him. He was not able to visualize how his spiritual gifts could fit into the rigid requirements of the job description of a senior pastor.

In seminary and as an associate, or in his first senior pastor position, the squeeze was accentuated to force him into shape and size to fit the perceived so-called ideal senior-pastor standard.

The church he serves, whatever the size, will have more unrealistic expectations of his ministry. The congregation's standard is for a man ten-feet-tall. Care for the church building as well as the people, visitation, community evangelism, committees, youth activities, Sunday school, and even social affairs somehow fall under his unwritten job description.

This man is a perfect setup for what happens next. Both the pastor and his church have imagined a role that is unreachable and untenable. He feels that he must not be a disappointment. He will become the ubiquitous pastor. One dictionary defines *ubiquitous:* ". . . existing or being everywhere, omnipresent."

Temporarily, verbal applause from the congregation will supply nourishment for his hungry ego with its human need of affirmation. They say: "I don't see how you do it all. You're always around. Mr. Everywhere. No matter how busy, you always make time."

In the end, a ubiquitous style of leadership is usually erosive and destructive to the effectiveness of such a pastor. Degenerative effects first puff him up, then burn him out.

Cecil Murphy, writing in the Minister's Workshop column of *Christianity Today,* cited a minister with a leadership style like this:

Gene became pastor of a congregation with a membership listed as nearly 600 but regular attendance of 125. Within six months, Gene had activities humming. Attendance picked up, new programs abounded. The budget doubled in three years. But in the fifth year, Gene moved to a different church. The church is back to an average attendance of 125, much like it was before Gene came on the scene. "In a lot of ways he hurt the church," a member said. "He kept everything in his grip. Nothing went on without his approval."[1]

His leadership style was based on an erroneous assumption—that the ministry was his. A scriptural injunction tells that ministry was intended to be the people's, and that the pastor is to train them. ". . . and some to be pastors and teachers, to prepare God's people for works of service, so that the body of Christ may be built up" (Eph. 4:11, 12).

When unscriptural and unrealistic expectations for ministry are lived out by the pastor and congregation, the ultimate effect will be erosive. The long-term health of the church will suffer.

This is particularly true when the shepherding life of a church is scrutinized. In the majority of situations, pastoral care and spiritual nurture of the congregation is exclusively the responsibility of the senior pastor. If his leadership style is ubiquitous, a vital part of his ministry will suffer neglect.

He will constantly be rediscovering that he cannot be everywhere at all times. A good pastor looks for ways to help his people grow, while numerous, urgent, but less important matters demand prime time. Their urgency may crowd out his central ministry of nurturing spiritual growth.

When the senior pastor usurps for himself the role of shepherding, there are short and long-range degenerative effects.

The laity is not prepared or equipped for works of service in building up the body as intended. The members are deprived of becoming the Lord's instruments of meaningful service. Their potential usefulness for God is stymied.

Those who would be served and nurtured suffer. With

1. *Christianity Today*, December 15, 1978, p. 32.

inadequate shepherding care, those in the body needing discipleship, encouragement, and exhortation fail to grow.

The ubiquitous pastor usually faces burnout after a ministry of five or six years. When a change of churches and pastorates appears to be his only solution for finding release from unbearable strain, he bails out and departs.

Termination is a terrible disservice because he leaves a shepherdless flock. He taught them to depend on him alone. Because he retained the exclusive right to shepherd, they are left unprepared to fend for themselves.

A transfer of confidence to another shepherd takes one-and-a-half to two years. Only then will the next pastor lead people into a nurturing relationship producing a similar rate of growth.

Warning words of Jesus should cause the pastor reconsideration.

> The hired hand is not the shepherd who owns the sheep. So when he sees the wolf coming, he abandons the sheep and runs away. Then the wolf attacks the flock and scatters it. The man runs away because he is a hired hand and cares nothing for the sheep (John 10:12, 13).

If a minister chooses to have a series of short pastorates, he must provide pastoral care in the congregations after he is gone.

A minister, who sees his primary gifts in areas other than shepherding, needs a source of people to minister as shepherds.

Care by a trained lay person may be more effective than by the senior pastor himself. The member needing nurture identifies more readily with a lay person than with a professional clergyman who may be regarded as too busy to spend extra time. If the pastor should leave for another church, the lay shepherds will be there to provide continuity. The laity will be blessed when in direct service as God's instruments.

In his book, *Everyone a Minister,* Oscar Feucht has observed rightfully:

> An adequate ministry is not a one man ministry. It is not even a corps of associated pastors. It is the whole church, congregation by congregation, mobilized and trained for mission. Only this strategy is adequate.[2]

2. Oscar E. Feucht, *Everyone a Minister* (Philadelphia: Westminster Press, 1974), p. 80.

1

Scattering Sheep and a Stressful Shepherd

My congregation had grown from 175 people to more than 600 in seven years. On paper it appeared to be a successful church. As the senior pastor, I was frustrated, overextended, and ready to resign.

My greatest strength had proved to be my undoing. God had given me a pastor's heart to care deeply for people. This intimate shepherding care had been a major factor in attracting people to the church. It continued as a catalyst for growth.

During these years, the church had become too much for me. The size of the flock had grown unwieldy for my style of ministering. I was caught in the scriptural parallel when Jethro advised Moses.

> What you are doing is not good. You and these people who come to you will only wear yourselves out. The work is too heavy for you; you cannot handle it alone (Exod. 18:17, 18).

Thousands of years later in Denver, Colorado, I couldn't handle it alone.

This modern-day Moses began to look to the senior pastors of Denver's largest churches. I wanted to learn how they had coped with the problem of adequate pastoral care for their growing congregations. In addition, I sent a questionnaire on the subject to each of the larger churches of my denomination.

Answers that I received were discouraging. Without exception, the replies indicated that as a congregation grew beyond three hundred to five hundred in numerical size, there was a decreasing pastoral care ministry.

Some families of our membership were scattering to other churches. The reason they gave was always the same, "The Mission Hills Church is getting too big. It's no longer the warm, intimate, caring church it was, back when we became a part of it."

They were right. I wavered on the verge of wanting to leave, too. I had a conviction that ideal shepherding was possible only in a smaller church. There was agreement with Carl S. Dudley, who wrote in *Christian Ministry:*

> A small church cannot grow in membership without giving up something very precious, the basic satisfaction that everyone knows or knows about someone else. This intimacy is not an accident, since the essential character of the small church is this capacity to know and care about others.[1]

I was ready to leave this larger, apparently successful church for a smaller one. If I couldn't handle it alone, I should resign.

My circumstances and my error have been described poignantly by Jay Adams.

> When the pastor on his own tries to do the work of an entire congregation . . . he fails because he spreads himself too thin, trying to do too much as one person. It is nothing

1. Carl S. Dudley, "Membership Growth, The Impossible Necessity." *Christian Ministry*, Vol. 8, No. 4, July, 1977.

less than pride for any one individual to think that he is capable of doing what God said is the work of an entire congregation. He fails also as a pastor-teacher. In spreading himself so thinly over the works of evangelism, as well as that of shepherding, and of teaching, he does none of those well. His sermons suffer, his members are not cared for, and even the fruit of the evangelism is minimal.[2]

I was being prepared to apply a lesson learned while ranching in Wyoming. God's plan was to change me from a shepherd to a ranch foreman.

My knowledge of the ways of sheep has provided background for sermon illustrations through the years. I had observed that God's people have many similarities to sheep. Now, I was to apply shepherding practices to my leadership as the senior pastor in a larger church.

The typical large sheep ranch in Wyoming divides its sheep into bands of one thousand ewes. Each band of ewes, with their lambs, is assigned to a solitary shepherd. These men, from Mexico, speak little English. They are given a trained sheep dog, a small sheep wagon in which they live alone, cook, and sleep.

Bands of sheep are dispersed on various sections of a ranch, with the location of each sheep wagon marking the bedding area for that flock. The sheep graze in the nearby grass. The wagon is located within traveling distance of a windmill. Sheep are herded there for water each day. At night they are bedded near the wagon, where the herder listens for coyotes and bands of wild dogs. After several days of feeding and browsing, the grass is grazed short, and it is time to move to greener pastures.

A large ranch has many bands of sheep. The ranch foreman manages the entire operation. It is his responsibility to oversee the shepherds with their dispersed bands. He checks the grass, locates a new grazing area, deter-

2. Jay E. Adams, *Pastoral Leadership* (Grand Rapids: Baker Book House, 1975), p. 25.

mines the distance from water, while arranging for the wagon's setting in a safe bedding ground. He instructs the shepherd in the care of the sheep, examining their health, progress, and general well-being.

The ranch foreman's style of leadership anticipates increase in the flocks. Numerical growth, production of wool, fat lambs that weigh well in the fall, are the money-making bottom line.

The shepherd views numerical growth from a different perspective than the foreman. A high rate of multiple births causes him frustration. He knows there is a limit to the number of sheep he can personally tend even if his workload is increased.

From my sheep ranch upbringing in Wyoming, there was a lesson for me. As the senior pastor of a suburban church, I had become a shepherd deeply worried about neglected and scattering sheep. I was ready to resign, while the Lord was readying me for reassignment. He was preparing me for a promotion on the same ranch. Soon I would begin to view myself in a different role.

2

Scanning for Assistance

In reflection, like the rapid recall of a drowning man, I came to realize that overextension had been accumulating for several years.

The effective performance for my intimate style of ministering peaked when the congregation reached 250 members. Shortly after, the time of stress began. My first response was to try harder. More hours were spent while efforts were increased. Leisure and family time were decreased. But this was only a temporary, stop-gap measure. Numbers of people needing a shepherding ministry continued to increase.

Next I went to seminars on time management. My response to overextension was to shape up, get more mileage out of my life! It was a helpful and needed discipline, but it did not meet the needs of our growing church. I kept reading and seeking advice.

The building of a multiple staff, in the form of seminary-trained professional clergymen, seemed the next logical step. I was assured that the added financial cost was really an investment that would soon take care of itself.

Any discussion of adding staff members brings up the question of finances. With an all-too-tight budget, how can a church even consider adding another staff member? . . .

Churches with a healthy growth pattern take an enlight-
ened step of faith. Their experience shows that a capable
staff member will result in more families that tithe. In two
years, the additional income will underwrite his salary and
an expanded program. So, church leaders trust the Lord and
challenge their people to provide the finances for the initial
salary.[1]

At the time I was facing my own personal crisis, I led
the church in seeking pastoral assistants. I gave considerable leadership to those selections. Search committees
explored the needs, looking for balance and complement.
We were forming a team. Finally we selected two men
gifted in particular ministries needed in the church. First,
we moved a seminary student, who had served as part-
time youth pastor, into a full-time minister of music/youth
pastor position. Then we hired a second man to serve as
Christian education/church administrator.

I had been convinced by counsel and reading that the
addition of more members to the pastoral staff would result in a shared shepherding ministry.

This was a wrong assumption. I soon discovered that
specialized associates do not necessarily contribute to the
pastoral-care ministry. Our new men activated the areas
where their gifts and talents were. Their assistance in pastoral care was minimal.

My young associates were gifted and motivated men.
They created new quality programs for their specialized
ministries. These attracted more people. My dilemma was
compounded by many more people who were being added
to our congregation. Each one needed pastoral care. This
modern-day Moses was overwhelmed.

I had not yet read the wise observation of Jay Adams.

. . . It may seem obvious that while there are advantages
(fellowship, the power of specialization, etc.) there are also

1. *Christianity Today,* March 24, 1978, p. 38.

disadvantages to a multiple staff ministry. Perhaps the greatest is this: thinking that the addition of specialized staff members itself will serve the needs of a growing large congregation. When "minister of music" . . . "of youth," and "of visitation," etc. are added, that does not necessarily mean that the congregation will be served better. . . . When a congregation reaches the size of 800-1000 members, it still does not receive adequate *pastoral* work by the addition of a "minister of music" or a "minister of youth." What is needed is the addition of three or four more "ministers of sheep!" It is a rare congregation that sees this and sufficiently provides for the need.[2]

While the general work of the church was enhanced by the addition of the gifted staff associates, the ministry of shepherding remained the responsibility of the senior pastor. My primary gift in this area caused other staff members to depend on me for this ministry.

I was convinced that the Holy Spirit gifts the leadership with the full complement of charisms needed to minister to the whole body. The logical step was to add individuals who were specialists in pastoral care because of gifts and training. This seemed the obvious move to take. It was consistent with my long-range goal for providing complete ministerial leadership as the church grew. I began to interview for a visitation pastor.

Two factors made me hesitate. In retrospect, I recognize them as God's providential leading. First was the *financial consideration*. Though the church was overextended financially, the need was great. Even one visitation pastor would only be Band-Aid treatment. I needed three or four full-time shepherds immediately.

The second reservation was received during the process of scrutinizing some of the larger churches in the Denver area. I observed a correlation between the addition of each pastoral staff person with a corresponding decrease in the

2. Adams, *Pastoral Leadership,* p. 55.

participation of lay people. *The increase of staff people was matched by a decrease in lay involvement.* I wondered if this contributed to the escalation of spectatorism in these larger churches.

We needed a church functioning as a *participatory* body, with each member active. This is the New Testament standard for a congregation. I was convinced that this was the type of church to minister spiritual health to people in a suburban community.

Now it is most apparent from Ephesians 4 that all Christians are "in the ministry." . . . When the ministry was thus left to the professionals there was nothing left for the people to do other than come to church and listen. They were told that it was their responsibility to bring the world into the church building to hear the pastor preach the gospel. Soon Christianity became nothing but a spectator sport, very much akin to the definition of football—22 men down on the field, desperately in need of rest, and 20 thousand in the grandstands, desperately in need of exercise![3]

I was left with one option. There remained a source for shepherding assistance, the laity of the Mission Hills Church.

I will be using the modern definitions of "laity" and "clergy." Today the term *clergy* is applied to one vocationally trained and employed in Christian ministry. When that vocational commitment ceases, even if he is ordained, he is no longer "clergy." The term *laity* is applied to the believer not financially reimbursed for his ministry.

Though this is the most prevalent understanding of these terms, such a distinction is not found in the New Testament.

The word "lay" goes back to the Greek word *laikos*. . . . It

3. Ray C. Stedman, *Body Life* (Glendale: Regal Books, 1972), pp. 78, 79.

means originally: belonging to the "*laos*"; that is the chosen people of God, both in the Old and New Testament.[4]

This term *laos* refers to all the people of God. Peter says: "But you are a chosen people, a royal priesthood, a holy nation, a people belonging to God. . . . Once you were not a people, but now you are the people of God" (1 Peter 2:9, 10).

In the New Testament sense all of God's people are his called people. They are God's "clergy" in the world.

The word "clergy" is derived from the Greek word *kleros*. . . . It is related to the verb "call" and is employed in the Greek New Testament when referring to the Holy Spirit calling a person by the Gospel into the Christian Fellowship of the church.[5]

Therefore, modern usage of the terms *laity* and *clergy* with their currently accepted meanings, have use only as functional terms. They have limited relationship to New Testament teachings. Usage must always be subordinate to biblical teachings of priesthood of all believers.

My remaining option for immediate shepherding assistance was the recruitment of lay people, who had demonstrated gifts of shepherding care. A step in that direction seemed a move away from dependency on the professional staff. We needed to stop the shift toward spectatorism occurring in the church. The New Testament teaching of the priesthood of all believers was our final benediction. Development of lay shepherds for a pastoral care ministry dovetailed perfectly with the priesthood of all believers.

Propositions for my plan of operation unfolded as a result of five conclusions:

4. Hendrick Kraemer, *A Theology of the Laity* (Philadelphia: Westminster Press, 1958), p. 49.

5. Feucht, *Everyone a Minister*, p. 57.

1. *All people, those in suburbia particularly, need the shepherding ministry of God.* They will respond to God through care extended to them by Christ's church in Christ's name.
2. *Spiritual growth is most productive in a caring community that provides pastoral leadership.* Nurture, feeding, and care are offered through adequate personal shepherding.
3. *Adequate shepherding care cannot be a one-man ministry.* It must be an apportioned, shared service. Part of the responsibility must be delegated to others. "Men who fear God, trustworthy men who hate dishonest gain" (Exod. 18:21).
4. *Most churches are financially unable to provide a large enough staff of associates to meet shepherding needs of the congregation.*
5. *There is a multiplicity of qualified lay persons with gifts related to the ministry of shepherding who can be a better source of competent pastoral service than a few staff members.* The volunteer status of the lay shepherd eliminates the idea that he is working for the congregation.

I had discovered the source of assistance at a very critical juncture in my pastoral career.

The process of my reassignment was now in its initial stages. God was unfolding his plan to broaden my horizons. He was going to make me a ranch foreman.

3

A Scheme for Lay Shepherding

I was beginning to look like a senior pastor. My hair had turned white, and character lines were becoming more deeply etched on my face. Overextension in my ministry seemed to contribute to all of this.

Finally, I concluded that the solo style of ministry simply wouldn't work in a larger church. Sharing the shepherding ministry with lay people seemed the correct course.

Numerous questions and necessary decisions crowded in. Who should be chosen? How many shepherds would be enough in the beginning phase? How should they be trained and mobilized?

The added responsibility of training others seemed overwhelming. Again I was tempted to think that it would still be so much easier to resign than remain.

The foundation for lay shepherding at the Mission Hills Church was laid in study and evaluation of similar programs in nationally prominent churches.

Dr. David Bailey, minister of pastoral care at Garden Grove (California) Community Church, invited me to be his houseguest. During those days I studied the well-organized Lay Ministers Pastoral Care Program of that superchurch.

During one interview, David Bailey described the role of lay minister in his church.

> Our entire pastoral care is designed to relate the people of the church to their Lay Minister. He is responsible to be in contact with them personally through visiting in their homes, telephoning, and personal letters. The Lay Minister is to be on the alert to greet the people assigned to him as he sees them in church. He is to notice the ones he does not see and contact them. The Lay Ministers are assistants to the Ministers in sharing the concern of Christ's church for each member.[1]

Garden Grove, like most churches studied, chooses its lay ministers by recruitment of volunteers. Candidates are placed in a training program; they can serve as lay minister interns while they study. Upon completion of the program, they receive the Certificate of Credentialed Lay Minister.

The Garden Grove program is organized on a geographic basis. Orange County plus parts of Los Angeles County are divided into zones. Member families are pinpointed in areas and assigned to a zone lay minister who lives nearby. He is responsible to each family. Quarterly contacts are suggested. Accountability is built into the system. The zone lay minister reports to a division lay minister, he to an area lay minister, who advises the salaried minister of pastoral care.

Calvary Temple of Denver, Colorado, has a similar program, called the Lay Shepherd Ministry. People are recruited or volunteer to serve. Attendance at a twelve-hour Laymen's Educational Advancement and Development Course is required. After that course is completed, the trainee is recognized as a lay shepherd.

The organizational structure of Calvary Temple's Lay-Shepherd Ministry is patterned after the Garden Grove program. The city of Denver is divided into geographic

---

1. Interview with David D. Bailey, Minister of Pastoral Care, Garden Grove Community Church, Garden Grove, California, January 26, 1979.

sectors. Accountability is achieved through a similar pyramid of supervision.

A different approach to lay shepherding is used by the Wooddale Baptist Church in the Minneapolis area. Within the larger church, small congregations are set up like the adult Sunday-school classes. Each small congregation has a teacher who functions as a pastor. These congregations are used as channels of communication for many activities of the church. They are centers of fellowship and spiritual growth, where people know and pray for each other.

In Whittier, California, Dan Baumann, former senior minister of the Whittier Area Baptist Fellowship, described a successful care ministry of that church:

> *Circles of Concern.* The Congregation is broken down into twenty-five circles which meet on a regular basis. Membership is voluntary; no one is forced to participate. Each circle averages about seven families who meet monthly for a study night. One month they gather in the twenty-five homes for Bible Study, discussion, sharing and prayer. The next month at church for a meeting of adults only. These sessions occur on Wednesday. A social night is conducted by each circle every month. The nature of the socials is determined by the individual circles. Groupings change each year to encourage people to make new friends and to cut down the likelihood of cliques. Circle leaders are chosen because of their commitment to a caring ministry. It is the responsibility of these individuals to pray for each member of their circle at least once a week, to lead the studies and socials, to keep in regular contact with all members . . . visit sick and delinquent members, and communicate emergent needs to the pastoral staff.[2]

I studied smaller churches as well. Don Fuller is the sole pastor of Grace Baptist Church in Anaconda, Montana. His wife is his personal secretary on a volunteer

2. Dan Baumann, *All Originality Makes a Dull Church* (Santa Ana: Vision House Publishers, 1976), pp. 107, 108.

basis. Grace Baptist averages one hundred people in worship services.

In the fall of 1976, this pastor organized nine teams each having a deacon and his wife. These teams lead nine prayer/share groups, which include nonmember families as well as member families. The husband, wife, and children are assigned to the same group. Each deacon with his wife has approximately ten households assigned to them.

The groups view their deacon and his wife as associates in ministry with the pastor. Weekly prayer/share meetings include children as well as adults. Groups select their own time and place of meeting. Different groups meet different nights of the week, and attendance varies from four to twenty. Everyone uses the prayer/share guide, written by Pastor Fuller, edited and mimeographed by Mrs. Fuller, and placed in the bulletin on Sunday.

I learned that shared shepherding isn't just for larger churches, where the senior pastor can no longer handle the pastoral ministry alone. It is a biblical principle of leadership which can multiply the effectiveness of a solo pastor in a smaller church. Don Fuller has become a ranch foreman in a church of 150 members. In reflection, I wish that I had learned these lessons earlier to use in the small churches of my earlier pastorates.

From research and study of these churches plus others, from extensive reading on care ministries and small groups, a plan for a lay-shepherding ministry was developing. God was showing me a schematic for Mission Hills Church.

Though I realized there were many varying philosophies, creative approaches, and differing ideas with respect to lay shepherding, it was now time to pick and choose. Questions arose that demanded decisions.

1. *Who were to be the lay shepherds?* It seemed wise to me to train people who had been elected by the congregation to offices that were associated with spiritual leadership. Deacons, rather than ones who might volun-

teer, seemed best positioned to train for a lay-shepherding ministry.

> The pastor is to be the initial enlister and trainer of his people until a new breed is ready to carry on that work. The best place for him to begin is with the existing leadership of the church—the elders and/or the deacons. These in turn will shortly thereafter reproduce themselves in the lives of others in the congregation. This might be costly at the onset, in terms of time and energy, but it will doubtless produce abundant and enduring fruit.[3]

Some years prior, a Coordinating Board composed of moderator, senior pastor, four board chairmen (including the deacon chairman), had been constituted as the executive board of the church. Therefore, the Board of Deacons was free to major in spiritual ministries. A minor change shifted the selection of deaconesses, so that those nominated had to be the wives of deacons. This ensured the necessary husband-wife combinations.

I settled on the term *Little Flock* as the formal name for each of the shepherding groups. In my thinking, there was a parallel between separating the people of the congregation into Little Flocks like the various bands of sheep under one herder on the Wyoming plains.

2. *What type of training was to be given?* To teach lay people what I had learned about shepherding from twenty-three years in the pastorate would take more than a few initial lessons.

I could see pouring my life into lay shepherds so they could share the ministry with me. The training would need to include formal teaching, on-the-job experience and an associational discipling with me. This would require a continual program, possibly weekly, for a good part of the year.

---

3. Synesio Lyra, Jr., *A New Laity* (Garden Grove, CA.: Lay Ministry Training Center), p. 13.

3. *Who should be included in the shepherding ministry?* The congregation who had used the adult Sunday-school class plan had many advantages. A primary disadvantage is that it did not extend to the entire membership. Non-Sunday-school attenders were excluded. Teachers and workers in other departments of the Sunday school could be reached in a limited manner.

The "circles of concern" plan has the same basic disadvantage. Including only those who volunteer to be a part of the ministry will miss a percentage of the membership. These, intentionally or by default, exclude themselves. Often reserved, timid, nongregarious people have more need for shepherding care and a support group than the natural joiners. They are reluctant to sign up to be a part of a new and unknown ministry.

I decided that Little Flocks should include every household in the church regardless of individual church membership or commitment to Christ. If everyone was to be included under the umbrella of shepherding care, assignment seemed the only workable procedure.

Each member family would be assigned to a Little Flock under the pastoral care of a designated husband-wife shepherding team. I knew that a small percentage of those assigned would probably be inactive in Little Flock functions. In spite of a reluctance to participate, these individuals would benefit by having a lay pastor and his wife to minister to them.

4. *How to determine the assignment of people to their respective Little Flocks was a difficult decision.* Because the Mission Hills Church ministers to a suburban area, most of the membership lives within a three-mile radius of the church. Forming the groups on the basis of geography was pointless. I knew that guidelines had to be relational, with careful formation.

Relationships needed to be vertical in respect to the lay-shepherd leadership and horizontal in reference to flock members. Interrelating as cohesion would determine whether the Little Flock would form a meaningful unit.

Should the shepherding group be homogeneous in composition? Should the singles, elderly, young parents, professionals, and blue-collar employees be placed in groups with others of similar circumstances and common interests? Or, should each Little Flock be a heterogeneous group, composed of people who represented a cross section of the congregation?

It seemed advisable to choose the latter option. We arranged to place in the Little Flocks people of all ages, differing income levels, dissimilar vocational pursuits, and varying marital status. This has required more effort for the husband/wife teams to effect relationships with unlike Little Flock members.

Time has proved this the correct course for many reasons. Single-parent mothers and their children had men and fathers in their Little Flock to relate to. Single and divorced people were included in family affairs. The elderly were brought into the mainstream of the church. This all outweighed the early difficulties in making each group a cohesive whole.

During the first year of the shepherding ministry, a measure of choice was given to church members. Each household received a mailed form with the names of the lay shepherds listed. Members were asked to circle the names of three deacons they could relate to. (Few realized the significance of the plans that were being made, and only 27 percent of the forms were returned.)

Lay-shepherding teams were asked to present the names of six member-households they would like to have in their Little Flocks. There was some duplication that had to be matched with requests from the returned forms.

I chose not to use a draft. A draft by deacons for shepherding group members would have created a climate of choosing up sides. Because the guidelines were relational, the selection required careful study and prayer.

After requests by the membership and the lay-shepherding teams were honored, the chairman of the Board of Deacons, the chairwoman of the Board of Deaconesses, and I finished the task. We spent several hours studying the remaining names and the composition of each Little Flock. We looked for balance.

Considerable prayer went into that final placement. After all, "Man looks at the outward appearance, but the LORD looks at the heart" (1 Sam. 16:7). Christ our Shepherd knew which lay shepherd could best minister to each of his sheep.

Approximately twelve households were placed in each Little Flock. Flocks including households representing single people were increased.

The basic plan was ready. The congregation and the lay shepherds had been initially prepared. The scheme for sharing the shepherding ministry was developing.

Study, planning, preparation, and prayer had started the transformation. I was excited. Everywhere I looked, I saw the potential of lay people with the opportunity of spiritual service for their God. My growing congregation had the prospect of receiving the shepherding it needed.

I was beginning to be a ranch foreman.

4

Training Shapes
Lay Shepherds

Deacon watch-care lists are not new in church circles. Usually they are mimeographed, assigned, and dutifully placed in the deacon notebook. The deacon is aware that he has a spiritual responsibility for the people assigned to him. Frequently, the list remains in the notebook and only occasionally pricks the conscience of the deacon.

I realized that the whole project might not go further than the composition of lists with their assignment to deacon-deaconess teams. How could I motivate the deacons and deaconesses into an active and meaningful lay-shepherding ministry?

Two things were necessary. First, I would model my own shepherding as an example. I needed to be the master teacher. Second, I would need to develop a trial-and-error process so that they could teach themselves. This required frequent exposure of my life to theirs. This would take a great amount of time and proximity.

I chose a weekly training period as the most practical means of pouring my experiences into the lives of trainees. The deacons and deaconesses met with me at church, in the fireside room, around tables, each Wednesday evening during the regular midweek service time. The lay-shepherd training class was designed in nine-month increments, from September through May.

At the time of the original edition, the training program was concluding its third year. As the program progressed, different approaches and emphases were required. Each training year revealed weaknesses requiring revision.

This chapter will give an overview of the lay-shepherd training of the first three years. Twelve husband-wife teams were enrolled in the first training year; sixteen in the second year of training; and nineteen teams were enrolled in the current year.

The First Year

The weekly ninety-minute class session was aimed at training the deacons and deaconesses. They were to become proficient in shepherding skills while they were developing their own ministries to their Little Flocks.

Minimum requirements for Little Flock ministry provided a standard for each shepherding team:

1. There must be a corporate Little Flock gathering at least once each three months.
2. There must be the establishment of a meaningful pastoral relationship between the lay shepherd and each member of his Little Flock.
3. A hospital call must be made by the lay shepherd on each Little Flock member who is hospitalized.
4. An undershepherding team, husband and wife from the Little Flock, must be selected and trained as assistants in the ministry of the flock.
5. A home-communion service, with the gathered Little Flock, is to be held in one of the homes at least once each year.[1]

1. Charles A. Ver Straten, "Changing Baptist Deacons Into Lay Shepherds" (Doctoral Dissertation, Denver: Conservative Baptist Theological Seminary, 1980), p. 104.

On-the-job training with its weekly sessions produced several indirect benefits. The first five minutes of the class period were spent in report time. Lay shepherds shared corporate activities of their Little Flocks; they told about ministries of note with individual members. There was built-in accountability in completing assignments. The necessity of having something to share stimulated the ministries.

The second five minutes of each training-class period were used for checking memorized verses with members (not their mates). Knowing one would be expected to recite to a fellow trainee was a good discipline and an effective spur. Frequent sharing by class members about new discoveries and developments in their devotional lives worked as a catalyst to others.

As the instructor, I wrote a notebook which became the training manual. It was a simple 5½-by-8½ inch, three-ring notebook bearing the name of the deacon or deaconess. All the printed materials were punched to fit the notebook. The deacons and deaconesses placed weekly handouts in designated sections. In three years of training, these notebooks have become valuable for reference and resource.

The notebooks contain seven sections: 1. Assignments; 2. Memorization; 3. Personal Growth; 4. Doctrine; 5. Little Flock Ministry; 6. How to Shepherd; and 7. Management Principles.

A summary of each section gives insight into the content of the first year's training program:

1. *Assignments.* This section received an update at the beginning of each three-month period of training. It listed the dates of the weekly meetings with exceptions, the memorization schedule, other assignments, and the general theme of each meeting.

2. *Memorization.* The Navigator's *Topical Memory System* was used. Verse cards were printed to be cut out and placed in each notebook. The New International Version was the translation used in the memory program and

the training class. Each trainee began memorizing with no advantages because of a previous memorization. Also, a new translation forced a fresh look at verses learned by rote in childhood. Some mature-appearing Christians began to admit years since they had committed any portion of the Bible to memory. They had been depending on a collection of verses memorized many years ago. Knowing they were expected to share their newly memorized verse each week with a fellow trainee spurred them to plant God's Word in their hearts and minds.

3. *Doctrine.* The necessity for instructing the lay shepherds and their wives in sound doctrine became evident in the initial stages of training. Modeling a life of godly character, as described in 1 Timothy 3, was not enough. It was not enough for the lay-shepherding team to provide a ministry of compassion. Paul instructed Timothy, "Watch your life and doctrine closely" (1 Tim. 4:16). If the people were to be true shepherds, it was important to understand truthful doctrine, to recognize error, and be able to instruct the people under their care.

> Be shepherds of the church of God, which he bought with his own blood. I know that after I leave, savage wolves will come in among you and will not spare the flock. Even from your own number men will arise and distort the truth in order to draw away disciples after them. So be on your guard! (Acts 20:28–31).

The doctrinal section for the first half of the training year was based on the twelve articles of faith in the church's statement.

1. The Word of God
2. The Trinity
3. God the Father
4. Jesus Christ
5. The Holy Spirit
6. Regeneration

7. The Church
8. Christian Conduct
9. The Ordinances
10. Religious Liberty
11. Church Cooperation
12. The Last Things[2]

One-half hour of each training period (twelve weeks) was designated for the study of each of the articles in successive order.

Each of the twelve deacons was assigned one doctrinal area at the beginning of a quarter. On a given date, the trainee taught his doctrinal subject under the supervision of the senior pastor. A handout was prepared by the trainee and printed by the church office for distribution.

I was amazed at the benefits and pleased with the results. The teacher-deacon learned more than his students because of the time spent in mastering the subject and preparing for the lesson. Twelve deacons became knowledgeable in twelve important biblical doctrinal areas. Another advantage was the attention given to the lesson because of identification with the student teacher. Though the deacons would have expected sound teaching from their senior pastor, they listened better to a fellow layman. I admitted that the student teachers spent more hours in preparation than I might have, therefore probably instructing more thoroughly.

This course of study caused the deacons and their wives to be more interested in doctrine. They were more aware of the various nuances in theological meaning on the contemporary religious scene.

4. *Personal Growth.* This section included material for the devotional prayer life of the lay shepherd and received a primary emphasis the first year. Prayer sheets with a place to record the request, date asked, and date answered, were in the notebook.

2. Appendix 1, "An Affirmation of Our Faith."

As the instructor, I strongly encouraged each shepherd to pray for the people of his Little Flock. I shared the importance of prayers of intercession and how to develop a ministry of prayer. Samuel's example and words were basic, "As for me, far be it from me that I should sin against the LORD by failing to pray for you" (1 Sam. 12:23).

InterVarsity's guidebook for daily devotions, *Quiet Time*,[3] was given to each shepherding team at the initiation of the program to foster systematic devotions in the lives of the lay shepherds.

For several months the following guide for using the Bible at daily devotional time was employed. Paragraph assignments in Scripture were made for each day so that the students and I would be using the same passage. A standard form entitled "Paragraph Title Record" was prepared.[4]

Each week's completed forms were handed in for checking. I penned affirming and encouraging notes on them when merited. These forms were returned, when those of the following week were collected.

Initially, there was minor resistance by some class members. A few of the trainees felt that I was looking over their shoulders during their devotional time. Others thought it was too mechanical and robbed them of spontaneity. Eventually, all the students were cooperative enough to comply. Those who initially resisted admitted later that it was a needed discipline.

Other devotional materials and techniques were used. When the daily quiet time was well established, the trainees were encouraged to develop their devotions in a manner that would assure spiritual growth.

5. *Little Flocks.* A listing of each of the Little Flocks appeared under its respective shepherding team. Each dea-

---

3. *Quiet Time* (Downers Grove: InterVarsity Press, 1977).
4. Appendix 2, Bible Reading. *See* a sample "Paragraph Title Record" form.

con and deaconess had a record of all the other Little Flocks and made additions as new members were assigned.

There were instructions about the selection, role, and duties, of the undershepherding lay teams. Each team was requested to select and recruit another husband-wife combination from their Little Flock. They would assist in the shepherding responsibilities of the group.

Undershepherds were invited to one weekly orientation meeting. They were told about the total shepherding program in general and the role of the undershepherds in particular. This group provided a reservoir of potential deacons and deaconesses who had been introduced to the Little Flock ministry.

Also included in this section were instructions in "Basic Requirements for Overseeing Your Little Flock."[5]

6. *How to Shepherd.* This was the practical section of the notebook. I wrote much of the material from my own ranch experience and from many years as a shepherding pastor. This was applied to lay shepherding, converted into the form of weekly handouts, and placed in the notebook. The notebook section "How to Shepherd," included the following studies.

1. The Shepherd is a *watchman*
2. The Shepherd is a *guard*
3. The Shepherd is a *guide*
4. The Shepherd is a *physician*
5. The Shepherd is a *rescuer*
6. The Shepherd is a *feeder of the sheep*
7. The Shepherd is a *lover of the sheep*[6]

As the first year of training progressed, handouts on evangelism, counseling in response to the invitation, hospital

5. Appendix 3, Little Flock Section.
6. C. Ver Straten, *Shepherding Notebook* (Littleton, Colo.: Mission Hills Baptist Church, 1979), "How to Shepherd" chapter.

visitation, and case histories for study were added to this section of the notebook.

7. *Management.* Because the ministry of shepherding involves a considerable amount of time, it seemed wise to introduce some basic management principles. The teams needed to learn to prioritize their lives to handle the additional stresses that were occurring. This section was minor in comparison to others, but I was surprised at the enthusiastic interest.

Summary: The hours I spent in preparing notebook assignments and contents in advance of the class were many, as was the costly effort required in actual classroom training, but it was time well spent.

> The wise pastor also recognizes that a vital part of his role as shepherd is the training of these lay shepherds. . . . This takes time but it is one of the most productive investments which the shepherd can make.[7]

The Second Year

Several changes transpired in the second year of training. In August we began with a two-day retreat to a condominium overlooking beautiful Lake Dillon.

The thrust of the year was *discipleship.* Course One and Course Two of the Navigators' *2:7 Series*[8] were used at each training session. Class sessions required about thirty-minutes preparation by trainees. Memory work and basic Bible study were included. Basic principles of discipleship for spiritual growth were stressed.

Monthly business meetings for the Board of Deacons and Deaconesses were moved to the third Wednesday night of each month. Previously, the meetings had been held on

---

7. Eugene L. Stowe, *The Ministry of Shepherding* (Kansas City: Beacon Hill Press, 1976), p. 132.

8. *The 2:7 Series* (Colorado Springs: Navigators, 1973).

the third Tuesday preceding the Wednesday night training class. That had caused a strain on the families of shepherding teams, resulting in absenteeism. The change was a welcome relief. Even though the training program had one less class each month, the benefits of meeting together were retained. The morale of the corps was heightened.

The Third Year

As the year began, the desire for spiritual renewal was a primary concern. If a deeper work were to happen in the lives of the lay shepherds, then prospects of a broad-based renewal would be bright.

The book *Celebration of Discipline*, by Richard Foster, has become the textbook of the year. One chapter a month is studied.

In September "The Discipline of Meditation," was read and discussed by each husband-wife team. The chairman of Deacons and his wife, chairwoman of Deaconesses, were assigned a ninety-minute seminar on meditation. They read everything available to them on the subject.

On the night of their co-teaching, I sat in amazement. The presentation was very professional. It was the best teaching I had ever heard on the subject. I learned much about Christian meditation I had never heard before.

My wife and I were teaching an evening class "Patterns for Christian Growth" at the seminary during this time. I asked Bill and Sharon Ward to bring a miniversion of their seminar to my class. The response of the class was electric. Hearing this lay-shepherding couple a second time, I marveled. The potential in lay people for spiritual teaching and leadership is often missed by overcommitted professionals.

The next month we continued Foster's material on "The Discipline of Fasting." The couple assigned to the seminar read nearly thirty books and pamphlets on the subject of fasting. They experimented with fasting, using different methods and durations through the month. The deacon completed one five-day fast. This team, Bob and Bev Maitan, brought quality teaching that people would travel and pay to hear.

I asked this couple to bring a miniversion of their seminar to the evening service prior to the monthly observance of the Lord's Supper. Many in the congregation became interested and excited about fasting in their own lives.

The deacons and deaconesses declared a twenty-four-hour fast before their next monthly business meeting. This fast was climaxed with prayer and sharing around tables in the fireside room. Everyone celebrated with a soup and fruit banquet.

Richard Foster's chapter on the "Discipline of Simplicity" was used in December. In our affluent community, this emphasis was timely. The seminar by Bob and Jan Burnside was most convicting. They suggested strong alternatives to those in which most of us are living.

As I walked home that evening, I reflected on lay people teaching lay people to choose a simpler lifestyle. No preacher in the world could have handled the subject as effectively as the credible and sincere couple who had been our instructors.

The third year of training featured Little Flock ministries plus a variety of other topics. The first Wednesday evening of the month became a team night.

On the first Wednesday in October, the deacon-deaconess teams were assigned a home visit to a Little Flock household. Teams who had children brought them to midweek programs at church, then made the home visit. A written report was handed in at the next week's class.

On the first Wednesday night in November each team dropped off children before driving to a quiet place. Communication and prayer for each other was primary. The shepherds were instructed to conclude their evening in conversational prayer for members of their Little Flock.

The assignment for December was to leave the children at the midweek service. This gave the lay shepherd time to take his wife to a restaurant for dessert and coffee. There they planned their family activities for the holiday season.

In addition to team night, workshops with specialists were conducted once a month. These were designed to equip the lay shepherds to minister in practical ways.

One night in September was designated as a Study Night. Position papers had previously been distributed. I led the deacons and deaconesses in: A Scriptural Study on Divorce; How to Handle Divorce in the Church; How to Care for the Divorcing and Divorced Person.

In October a member who does financial planning presented a simple nonaccounting plan for money management. This might be taught to Little Flock households willing to have help.

Each year of lay-shepherd training has had strengths and weaknesses, but progress has been made. There was a general consensus that our handle on something good had just begun.

5

Lay Shepherds Develop Their Style

The training sessions were designed to develop shepherd-leaders. Conformity in ministry was not intended. I believe that the Holy Spirit gives unique combinations of gifts to the servants he is equipping. Innovation and creativity were encouraged in the program. Different styles soon emerged becoming a trend which continues.

The training classes were designed to remind shepherds-in-training to keep God's purpose before them. The purpose must be identical with that of the Great Shepherd. The lay shepherd's role is not merely to "keep" people with Christ, but also to "develop" them for Christ's service. The objective is not *maintaining* people, it is *nurturing* them.

The functions of pastoral care are well-defined by Clebsch and Jaekle:

1. *Healing* is that function in which a representative Christian person helps a debilitated person to be restored to a condition of wholeness, on the assumption that this restoration achieves also a new level of spiritual insight and welfare.
2. *Sustaining* consists of helping a hurting person to

53

endure and to transcend a circumstance in which restoration to his former condition or recuperation from his malady is either impossible or so remote as to seem improbable . . . but it goes beyond mere resignation to affirmation as it attempts to achieve spiritual growth through endurance of unwanted, or harmful, or dangerous experiences.

3. The pastoral function of *guiding* consists of assisting perplexed persons to make confident choices between alternative courses of thought and action, when such choices are viewed as affecting the present and future state of the soul. . . .

4. The *reconciling* function seeks to re-establish broken relationships between man and fellow man and between man and God . . . reconciling employs two emphatic modes of operation which we call forgiveness and discipline.[1]

This last reconciliation of man with God's forgiveness, is the evangelistic responsibility of the shepherd. To use a metaphor from the world of sheep, this could be termed, "lambing." In Wyoming sheep ranching, lambing is the bottom line. The amount of profit is determined by the size of the lamb crop. Likewise, if pastoral care excludes the lambing/evangelistic process, it has degenerated into a maintenance ministry. The importance of lost sheep is discovered in the words of the Great Shepherd:

Suppose one of you has a hundred sheep and loses one of them. Does he not leave the ninety-nine in the open country and go after the lost sheep until he finds it? . . . there is more rejoicing in heaven over one sinner who repents than over ninety-nine righteous persons who do not need to repent (Luke 15:4–7).

1. William A. Clebsch and Charles R. Jaekle, *Pastoral Care in Historical Perspective* (Englewood Cliffs: Prentice Hall, 1964), pp. 8, 9.

In the past, during the weekly training session, the first seven minutes have been used as a sharing time for lay shepherds. New activities and ministries were reported at that time. Occasionally, new ideas and approaches for effective shepherding have led into a natural brainstorming period. When this happened, the planned formal training was set aside for another week.

Periodically, "Report Forms of Little Flock Ministries by the Shepherding Teams" have been filled out and presented to the pastor-instructor.[2] The information that follows, describing the "on-the-job" training, is drawn from those reports.

The Social Life of the Church

The Sunday-school classes had been the primary source of social contact, but an increasing number of people not in Sunday school were on the outside. The social and fellowship life of the church began to incline in the direction of the Little Flocks. This was a change.

Because the lay-shepherding program began officially on July 1, it was an ideal time of year for backyard barbecues, patio gatherings, and picnics. The fireside room of the church was booked regularly on Sunday after church for cooperative buffets of Little Flock gatherings.

This flurry of activity began to acquaint people with others in the church. Almost immediately a warming trend was observed in the congregation. There was more visiting in the narthex of the church as people lingered longer after services. Reports drifted in that new friendships were being formed. Groups of couples were getting together outside the framework of the church.

2. Appendix 4. *See* sample "Report Form of Little Flock Ministries by the Shepherding Teams."

One report described a Halloween party for families of a Little Flock in the fireside room.

> There were forty in attendance at our Halloween party (dinner and games). The food for our covered-dish dinner was terrific. We must have the best cooks of the entire church in our Little Flock. It was good for my wife and me to watch the families eating together. We learned a lot about them by just watching. Almost everyone was in a Halloween costume. A "best" costume was chosen from each group as men, women, boys, and girls modeled their outfits. Our game time was for the entire family. Our Little Flock saw families together and began to get acquainted with each other as family units. As deacon and deaconess, we began to think of our Little Flock as whole families instead of just the adults.

Considerable creativity began to surface as the lay shepherds were encouraged to develop their own styles of ministry:

> Because pastors and elders recognize . . . the need for fellowship among the members of their congregations . . . an attempt will be made to encourage both formal and informal fellowship among the members. Creatively, they will think of ways in which to bring members of the congregation together to know one another *as human beings*, not merely as the persons who sit across the room in meetings.[3]

Prayer Meetings

Several Little Flocks held regular prayer meetings in which there was a sharing of requests and needs. Prayer was for those present as well as members who were absent. One Little Flock held a Bible study in the home of its

3. Adams, *The Pastoral Life*, p. 79.

shepherding team alternate Tuesday evenings. A report from that group reads:

> We have been studying 1 Peter two nights a month on Tuesday evenings at our house. There are about ten to twelve who come on a regular basis. We've enjoyed it. And our meeting has provided a sharing in spiritual matters. My wife and I are beginning to feel that we are spiritually ministering to our people.

The summer midweek ministry was assigned to the deacons who coordinated with the Little Flock ministry. Three "prayer-share" meetings were held on Wednesday nights in the home of deacons and their wives. Four shepherding teams with their Little Flocks were assigned to each gathering. These teams met together on a rotating basis in the homes of the deacons assigned. Deacons took turns as leaders of the gatherings. Planning took into consideration vacations of those involved.

The summer midweek program proved to be an excellent on-the-job training experience. It gave the lay shepherds an opportunity to teach and lead prayer meetings. We concluded that it was the best midweek summer program the church had had.

Building Relationships

As relationships began to form between the shepherding teams and members, opportunities occurred for personal counseling. Sometimes this was a slow process. At one class session, a deacon asked,

> How can we get people to open up to us? We have one family on our list that's so private and reserved, we never get beyond "Hello! How are you?" When we have visited

in the home, it gets uncomfortable and awkward. How do you get into spiritual matters?

On the spur of the moment, I suggested a technique I've used frequently. "I ask them, 'when I pray for you and for the members of your family, what can I pray for . . . how should I pray?' "

Two weeks later, during the Little Flock sharing period of the weekly class session, the same deacon raised his hand.

> The advice the pastor gave works like a top. We couldn't believe it. My wife and I visited our "closed-do-not-enter" family. It was the same strained situation. Then, just before we were getting ready to leave, and I wanted to pray, I said: "We pray for each family in our Little Flock each week. When we pray for each member of your family, what should we pray for?" We couldn't believe what happened next. The woman began to tell about their teenage daughter and the boyfriend who wasn't a good influence. They spoke of their concern about the junior high son who didn't want to go to church anymore. For the first time, we started to get into their lives. And all that happened when you gave us that simple question, Pastor!

Relationships that developed in the lay-shepherding teams helped people turn toward their lay shepherds for personal counsel.

As the senior pastor, I struggled with the shifting dependency of church members from me to others. I discovered something unhealthy in me that wanted people to need me more than anyone else. I grew up a little in the process. Because of the close involvement with the lay shepherds, the relinquishing process was easier.

I realized I was no longer the indispensable confidant in our congregation. Giving up this role for a man who delighted in being the pastor-shepherd marked the final translation from shepherd to ranch foreman.

Ministering to the Ill

During a six-month period, thirty-eight hospital calls were recorded by the shepherding teams. These provided relationships between the deacons, deaconesses and families under their care. Deaconesses often provided meals to the family at home during the hospitalization.

One deaconess's ministry is recorded in notes I jotted for my file.

One of our single women in her middle-aged years was hospitalized with a very painful kidney-stone condition. Surgery was necessary, and her deaconess and I were together with her for prayer before surgery. I was impressed when the deaconess said to the woman, just before she was taken to surgery, "Now I want you to know that I'm going to be down in the waiting room while you're in surgery. I'll be praying for you there. When it's all over, I'll represent you as family when the surgeon comes out, and I'll tell you everything he says when you are conscious."

When I visited the recovering patient two days later, she said: "Pastor, you have no idea what it meant to a single person like me to hear someone say: 'I'm going to represent you as your family to the doctor.'" Tears came, and then she said: "I feel more a part of the family at Mission Hills than I did before."

Another ministry of caring for physical needs in the congregation is prayer for healing. When there is a need, someone will request a prayer service. The fifth chapter of James has been used as a guideline for praying for the sick.

Is any one of you sick? He should call the elders of the church to pray over him and anoint him with oil in the name of the LORD. And the prayer offered in faith will make the sick person well; the LORD will raise him up (James 5:14, 15).

Throughout the years God has honored the prayer of faith by deacons who have gathered to pray.

In the second year of lay shepherding, Alice Halbrook sustained severe eye damage in a youth activity. She and her husband, plus teenage daughters, have had a ministry as youth sponsors. In a straw fight on a hay ride, straw struck her eye, detaching the outer layer.

After the injury, the layer would adhere temporarily then become detached. Many doctors and specialists were consulted. They agreed that no surgery could effect a permanent cure.

When detachment occurs the patient must have complete bed rest, with a patch over the affected eye and the other eye at complete rest. The patient must remain immobile for one week until attachment has taken place again.

This vivacious lady, with her effective youth ministry and Bible study to women, required one week out of four in bed for complete rest. She never knew when a detachment would occur. Planning anything was very tentative. Her life looked bleak.

Alice had an intense desire to be healed in order that he would be glorified. A deaconess told her that she believed God wanted to heal her. The inner witness grew.

There was fear that if she requested a prayer service for healing, and the Lord chose not to answer, the faith of young people would be shaken. Finally she was compelled to "ask."

Prayer services for healing are small, quiet gatherings including the ill, family members, deacons, and one or two pastoral staff persons. Alice asked if those who were such a part of her life could be present. Before the prayer service, she told them that if the Lord chose not to heal her she would love him as much as if he did.

We gathered in the fireside room with fifty young people, family members and friends. I instructed participants in the promise of James 5. The deacons and I knelt around

Alice who was kneeling at a chair. I anointed her with oil; we laid hands on her, praying earnestly with faith that he gave us.

These shepherds were ministering to a sheep with a physical need. The Great Shepherd extended his unseen hand through the hands of his undershepherds. "The prayer offered in faith will make the sick person well. . . . The prayer of a righteous man is powerful and effective" (James 5:15, 16).

Aware of his presence we arose, with an unusual calm measure of confidence, fringed with a question mark.

From that day Alice has not experienced another detachment of the top layer of that eye. She gives God the glory for his healing power. Hers is a vital life of touching many people for her Lord.

Evangelism

The shepherding ministry led to the salvation of some in the Little Flocks. One young member of the church had a wife who was not a Christian. She consented to attend church with her husband. The family, because of his membership, was assigned a deacon and deaconess in preretirement years. The deaconess nurtured the young wife with numerous expressions of care.

She reported an incident that might have thwarted her plan to bring the young wife into the kingdom.

We were received with a warm welcome. We chatted on for a short time about generalities, then said, "We have really come to share God's Word on this visit." The couple quickly found their Bibles, and we asked the young wife to read several salvation texts. . . . We suggested that she insert her name in the place of "whoever" in John 3:16. Tears flowed as she started to read this verse, and she quickly left the room. When she returned she apologized for crying. We answered, "The Lord loves a broken heart and a contrite spirit." Then we had a few words of encouragement to share the workbooks we left for a dual Bible study. The book by Rosalind Rinker on prayer was well received. We told them that the Lord's love was far greater than our love. My husband prayed for them.

Although this visit resulted in an emotional scene, the sowing of that seed of the gospel was rewarded in a harvest. Several months later the same deaconess wrote:

> The most thrilling incident in our Little Flock ministry for me was leading this dear little mother and wife to Christ in friendship evangelism. On the Sunday evening at the close of the Harold Carlson meeting many had gone forward to pray. The young husband was there, but I noticed his wife a couple of pews ahead of us standing alone. I slipped out of our pew and stood beside her and asked: "Would you like to pray?" She threw her arms around me, and we went forward and knelt at the altar, and she prayed to receive Christ . . . a little lamb come home.

Material Provision

A caring ministry for material needs has often been supplied through the program.

For years the church had received a deacon fund offering for the needy at the close of the monthly communion service. The offering was a few dollars to be used when dire circumstances arose. It was an unimportant matter in the life of the church. A Puritan work ethic guided our attitude. The smugness in most of our lives suggested, "God helps those who help themselves."

During the second year of the program something began to happen that changed this attitude. Each time the deacon offering was received, hundreds of dollars were counted.

The money came from a broad base of the membership. The deacons and pastoral staff were dumbfounded.

Recently it was reported that over twenty-five hundred dollars was in the deacon fund. Like Elijah's jug of oil, the more that was poured out, the more was replaced.

The question before the lay shepherds was thought provoking. "If Jesus were in our midst, whom would he help?"

Members were now viewed from a different perspective. We could see that the church had ministered to spiritual needs alone. The blindness referred to in the Book of James had been the indifferent, uncaring stance of the church.

> Suppose a brother or sister is without clothes and daily food. If one of you says to him, "Go, I wish you well; keep warm and well fed," but does nothing about his physical needs, what good is it? (2:14–16).

Practices of the early New Testament church began to live again in the midst of this modern church.

> There were no needy persons among them. For from time to time those who owned lands or houses sold them, brought the money from the sales and put it at the apostles' feet, and it was distributed to anyone as he had need (Acts 4:34–35).

The eyes of the lay shepherds were opened to see material needs in numerous lives. Several unemployed in the congregation had suffering families. We developed a new dimension of shepherding care that has continued until the present.

The lay shepherd is in close contact with the families of his Little Flock. He and his wife seek to be sensitive, wise, and good stewards. When they become convinced that financial help should be extended in Christ's name, the deacon confers with the chairman of the Board of Deacons. They decide if a gift should be given in cash or substance (because I often have intimate knowledge, they ask me to ratify the decision).

The lay shepherd delivers the check or produce to the family. There is an opportunity for prayer. The result is appreciation from a family that has received a visit from a ministering angel. Often a deepened relationship between a lay shepherd and sheep results.

Some people in the Little Flocks are chronically in financial straits, due to poor management. To bail them out at every turn wouldn't be helpful. Lay shepherds soon discovered that defeat with money management results in spiritual defeat. Counsel in better financial management, practical suggestions for budgeting, and assistance in prioritizing long-term financial objectives has become another aspect of ministry.

A few vignettes of caring help to Little Flock members illustrate this program.

A widow with several children received her final tax notice, with the date the property would be listed for sale. The lay shepherd comforted the apprehensive family. After counsel with the Board of Deacons, payment of taxes was approved, and paid in full. That woman saw the love of Jesus through a church called by his name.

Two graduated seminary couples were eking out survival in an effort to begin a new Christian music ministry. Their cupboards were bare. Two hundred dollars for groceries was granted each couple. Their lay shepherd, a grocery distributor, took them to a wholesale warehouse to let them shop for themselves. After three years of scrimping in seminary plus a scantier year, the young women were ecstatic. One declared, "It has been years since I've had so much fun. This is going to be the best Christmas ever at our house!"

A member whose mother had died had no money to travel for the funeral. An alert lay shepherd arranged for a check. He was greeted in the grieving home as though he were a visiting angel. He was.

When Christ is Lord in his church, he ministers materially through his people. Needs are met that arise in the lives of others in his care. Ronald Sider noted that God identified with the poor.

> . . . The Sovereign of the universe identifies with the weak and destitute . . . only in the incarnation can we begin dimly to perceive what God's identification with the weak, oppressed and poor really means. ". . . though he was rich," St. Paul says of our Lord Jesus, "yet for your sakes he became poor . . ." (2 Cor. 8:9).
>
> He was born in a small, insignificant province of the Roman Empire. . . . His parents were too poor to bring the normal offering for purification. Instead of a lamb, they brought two pigeons to the temple. Jesus was a refugee (Matt. 2:13–15) and thus an immigrant in Galilee (Matt. 2:19–23). Since Jewish rabbis received no fees for their teaching, Jesus had no regular income during his public ministry. Nor did he have a home of his own. He warned an eager follower who promised to follow him everywhere, "Foxes have holes and birds of the air have nests, but the Son of Man has no place to lay his head" (Matt. 8:20). Jesus also sent out his disciples in extreme poverty (Luke 9:3; 10:4). . . . Only as we feel the presence of the incarnate God in the form of a poor Galilean can we begin to understand his words: "for I was hungry and you gave me food, I was thirsty and you gave me drink, . . . I was naked and you clothed me, . . . Truly, I say to you, as you did it to one of the least of these my brethren, you did it to me" (Matt. 25:35–40 RSV).[4]

Other Lay Ministries

The lay shepherds shared a collective ministry while pursuing and developing their own styles of pastoral care.

4. Ronald J. Sider, *Rich Christians in an Age of Hunger* (Downers Grove: InterVarsity Press, 1977), p. 69.

One couple had an unusual telephone ministry with the members of their Little Flock. Another deaconess wrote notes of encouragement to the women she was shepherding. A lay shepherd had breakfast weekly at a local restaurant with different men from his shepherding group.

One deaconess, who had a special touch with teenagers, made burger dates with different young people from her Flock. She ministered effectively in many lives. One shepherd recruited the men to work in building a room on the small house of an elderly widow in his group.

The innovation and creativity that surfaced became very practical pastoral care.

6

Care Catalyzes a Church

William Fletcher, in his doctrinal thesis *A Caring Model for the Local Church*, observed:

> The place to begin is in the Christian community. Pastor and people must learn to care, first for one another, then for those outside. Helping a few to care is a start toward a caring community.[1]

The primary purpose of initiating the lay-shepherding program was to provide adequate pastoral care to everyone. Development of a sharing support group through Little Flocks was a second thought. To create a caring community was beyond my faith and vision. It is happening. Active love is contagious, growing with use. Our use of love to others allows us to receive an increasing measure from him. This is aptly described as the song "Pass It On" says, "It only takes a spark to get a fire going, and soon all those around can warm up in its glowing."[2]

Lay shepherds and wives became instruments of Christ's compassion and care; they became catalysts in creating

---

1. William M. Fletcher, *A Caring Model for the Local Church*, A Report of the Professional Project (Denver: Conservative Baptist Seminary, 1979), p. 2.
2. Kurt Kaiser, *Hymns for the Family of God*, "Pass It On" (Nashville: Paragon Associates, Inc., 1976), p. 641.

a climate. An entire congregation became a caring community.

Examples and illustrations are in order. In a public announcement, I asked those who had benefited to describe the ministry in writing. This resulted in numerous case histories of extended pastoral care. I share some of these.

Case Studies

A wife and the mother of four children, and a member of the church for many years has written:

"The most memorable time in my experience with real care was after our fire. Our house had been burning, and the firemen had just put it out. My neighbor, also a Mission Hills member, had called the prayer chain of the church.

"As I was stumbling through a tour of my blackened house, many of my church friends began to pour into my yard. The chairman of the Deacon Board was prompt to bring one hundred dollars from an emergency fund. I felt as if we were destitute.

"Caring Christians were saying: 'You're welcome to stay at our house tonight.' Others verbalized our thoughts: 'Where are you going to go?'

"Suddenly the voice of my deaconess took charge, almost ordered me: 'You will come to our house tonight.' Somehow she knew I couldn't make a decision. I needed a clear order!

"By the time we got there the house was loaded with bags of clothes, hangers of clothes, toys for the children, and money. Generosity and goodness came from all over the church. When I reflect back on that memorable day, my deaconess stands out!"

A lovely middle-aged woman who has undergone an unwanted divorce said:

"Going through this painful divorce has brought me to my knees in constant prayer for guidance. The one bright spot has been my ministering deacon and deaconess, George and Mary Jo Hockman.

"She has taken me to lunch many times. There she listened to my grieving and sorrowing with a concerned and loving heart. They invited me to be their guest for a weekend last summer at their cabin in the Rocky Mountain National Park. It was a weekend of sharing and caring in prayer. They were the most peaceful days; the only enjoyable days of the entire year.

"Their love just wrapped me up and made me glow for days afterward. Truly God has been good in sending to me his ministers of mercy."

A husband and father was hospitalized and underwent a very precarious surgery. His wife shared:

"We arrived home after the horrendous day of surgery. The three of us (mother and two teenage daughters) were weary and drained. Norma, our deaconess, had prepared and delivered to us the most lovely meal.

"It wasn't really necessary. The women of the house weren't hospitalized. We could have cooked. But it was just wonderful to sit down to a prepared meal after one of the worst days of our lives. We felt so loved, that someone cared to meet our needs at such a late hour."

A divorced mother who bore the entire financial brunt of rearing three small children told of a bright chapter in her life:

"It's so hard making ends meet around this house. With me in school, and the kids to provide for, there is never any extra left over.

"I couldn't believe it when my deaconess wanted to take me shopping for a new outfit for Christmas. She and her husband decided this was what they wanted to give to

Jesus on his birthday. It meant so much to me. She has been a real help in discipling me since I accepted Christ.

"But to give me a gift for Jesus made me understand Christmas and Christianity a whole lot better."

Karen Kasch's brother Ron was diagnosed as being in the advanced stages of Hodgkin's disease. Ron was twenty-three years of age and not a Christian. Karen, in the early stages of pregnancy, traveled over two hundred miles to visit him in the hospital. While there, she began to miscarry and was hospitalized. Karen's husband Russ phoned his deacon, Mel Anderson, for prayer. The roads were a solid sheet of ice, but the sound of Russ's voice on the phone was disturbed and frantic.

After prayer, Mel and Judy decided that they were needed during this difficult time. They drove the icy road to the hospital, where they ministered to Russ and Karen.

Then Mel visited Ron on another floor of the hospital. He led him to a saving knowledge of Christ. Ron's father commented on the difference. A lost sheep was brought into the fold.

Mel and Judy returned home after an exhausting and eventful day of shepherding.

A mother of a grown son and three teenage daughters described what shepherding care meant to her during the difficult days of divorce:

"On January 11, 1979, my small secure world fell apart when my husband chose to leave. I was suddenly faced with almost total responsibility for the support of three daughters and the bills of running a household. Three months before I had been involved in a serious multicar accident. I was facing a series of corrective surgeries.

"I felt very alone and helpless. My deacon and deaconess, Harry and Carol Schanker, as well as the shepherding group, ministered in a number of loving and practical ways.

"For a period of time, I had no income so that my meager savings were exhausted. I was able to provide only the least expensive soups, beans, and potatoes for my children.

"Our shepherding group, under the Schankers, made a point to open their homes for dinner. They included us in their families many times.

"I received anonymous financial help as well as food and assistance. Neither my daughters nor I ever felt like we were someone's 'responsibility'; only that we were loved and hurting family members.

"My lay shepherds loved us, prayed with us, hurt with us, and cried with us. They were as close as my telephone. When I did not call them, they called me.

"As a woman alone, with overwhelming family and financial responsibilities, I needed practical advice and constant encouragement. Help was needed in every area, from necessary home maintenance to college financing. Harry and Carol spent hours helping me reach career and financial decisions.

"Each time I was hospitalized, the Schankers were there. While hospitalized and during recovery, our shepherding group provided food, transportation, and extra tender loving care.

"The past three years have been a time of stress and turmoil, but also a time of great personal growth. The encouragement, love, and support of my shepherds, as well as other dear Christian friends, has kept my life together. I cannot read Matthew 25:35–40 without seeing the members of my 'family,' and my shepherds."

A deacon heard via the grapevine that the children of a black family in his Little Flock were hurt by peers' needless racial slurs and jokes. The deacon took their mother to lunch to hear the story.

He proceeded to initiate procedures in three youth groups to teach corrective measures. In one of the classes fellow students were visibly moved. The situation was corrected. Those involved learned lessons of sensitivity to the potential poison of the human tongue.

A divorced woman was plagued with breaking and entering of her house by her former mate. He knew which screens to take off. The windows were opened and things were missing from time to time. Two deacons spent an entire Saturday making the house secure. To that grateful woman's relief, there were no problems after that. Her home became a place of safety and refuge.

A young deaconess has felt the pressures of an unemployed husband. She wrote to the Board of Deaconesses what the chairwoman has meant to her as shepherdess.

"Our deacon and deaconess are Bill and Sharon Ward. We have never met more fantastic people. They are tremendous in their spiritual knowledge and practical insight. They are generous, thoughtful, kind, and available.

"I have never called Sharon with a problem that she didn't have time to help me. I've called her a lot this past year because I've been discouraged. She has taken hours to listen to me, to help me find answers. She doesn't just throw out some quick, nice-sounding, Christian platitude. She always takes time to share from her life and to find appropriate scripture for the need.

"Yet, I must add that she and Bill are so humble, human, and reachable. I never felt that they put themselves up as some great authority. They are quick to mention their weaknesses. We never felt that we alone had all the problems and areas of defeat. They gave us the impression that we are all in this together. We could help each other.

"Bill and Sharon have obviously meant so very much to us. They are exceptional. We, like the others, are seeking to do our best, but they have gone above and beyond the call of duty."

Ruth Herder was widowed. Her husband, Dean, had been a leader and deacon of the church. Ruth was left with four children ranging from elementary to high school in age. She and her family exemplify a modern-day recognition that the care of widows and their children are the responsibility of the church. "Religion that God our Father accepts as pure and faultless is this: to look after orphans and widows in their distress . . ." (James 1:27). Ruth reflects on care extended to her and to the children through these years:

"As a widow, the male authority and influence of husband and father is missing. I look to God and his church (through the senior pastor and deacons) to care for my family both spiritually and in physical and material ways, too.

"Paul and Kaye Norlander have been our faithful deacon and deaconess. During the years my family was in their Little Flock, they helped us in so many different ways.

"I was so bewildered when it was necessary to change houses. They moved us, arranging for helpers, moving furniture and working long hours to get the job done.

"As I look back on it now, I think I just stood around being in the way. Without a husband, insecurity and fear sometimes overwhelm. My lay shepherds, both of them, gave much time, to meet and talk. Our family was invited to their home for ice cream and many social gatherings. They remembered us at Thanksgiving and Christmas with enough food for a feast.

"Paul gave endless financial advice. He spent hours going over my records, compiling back data, going to an attorney and a CPA, to file back income tax statements.

"When there were emergencies he arranged financial help through the deacon fund. He made minor car repairs, and then loaned me a car while mine was being fixed. He made home improvements and repairs when they were needed.

"A neighbor was drinking too much and threatened my family. We were all very afraid. I called the Norlanders who came immediately in response to the call.

"Others from our church family have helped in so many different ways. A number of families frequently give me money. Many have included us in their families. They warm our lives."

A further incident in this family's life warmed my heart. Laura, the second daughter, was having her first date. She planned for the big evening with detail and anticipation. With considerable sadness she shared with her mother one great regret: her dad wouldn't be there to answer the door, meet her date, and wait with him before she made her grand entrance. They decided that "her" shepherd would be asked to stand in for her father. So Paul Norlander, lay shepherd, was Laura's father figure on that very important night.

Church Body—Catalyzed to Care

Ray Stedman described a quality of church life that was beginning to unfold at Mission Hills.

What is terribly missing is the experience of "body life"; that warm fellowship of Christian with Christian which the New Testament calls *koinonia,* and which was an essential part of early Christianity. The New Testament lays heavy emphasis upon the need for Christians to know each other, closely and intimately enough to be able to bear one another's burdens, confess faults one to another, rebuke, exhort, and admonish one another, minister to one another with the word and through song and prayer, and thus come to comprehend "with all saints" as Paul puts it, "What is the breadth and length and height and depth, and to know the love of Christ which surpasses knowledge" (Eph. 3:18, 19 rsv).[3]

The shepherds seem to represent the heart of the body. They reflect God's compassion and mercy. When they care, life is pumped to the entire body. Care is not primarily an emotion, it is an act of compassion. The will decides to care.

It has been observed that a church eventually reflects the personality of a pastor. He gives leadership in subtle, indirect ways in addition to active leadership.

A very gregarious pastor resigned. His church was a spontaneous, uninhibited fellowship that had been formed under his leadership. The minister following him was a quiet-mannered scholar with reserved qualities.

I visited the church a year after the new leader had begun his ministry. The mood and atmospheric change was notable.

This is not as evident in a larger church where direct contact with the senior pastor is limited. Different staff members and lay leaders share in influencing congregational attitudes and personality.

In our church, qualities of compassion and concern were translated through lay shepherds to the congregation. Shepherding care became the single most important thrust. Ministering care and concern became the hallmark of Christianity in our midst. We were becoming a caring church.

The apostle Paul emphasizes:

If I speak in the tongues of men and of angels, but have not love, I am only a resounding gong or a clanging cymbal. If I have the gift of prophecy and can fathom all mysteries and all knowledge, and if I have a faith that can move

3. Ray C. Stedman, *Body Life* (Glendale: Regal Books, 1972), p. 107.

mountains, but have not love, I am nothing. . . . the greatest of these is love (1 Cor. 13).

As the senior pastor, my primary efforts were spent in
pouring my shepherd's heart and life into laymen. We developed the program of shepherding so that all bases would
be covered.

Lay shepherds became the catalysts of change to the
congregation. They pumped love to the extremities of the
church body.

Reviewing this progress, I recognize that the emphasis
created a temporary lack of balance. Evangelism and
Christian education did not receive sufficient emphasis.

In the third year of training, corrective measures were
taken to balance our emphases.

I remain convinced that Christ led our building of his
church in this place. He desired to shepherd it into his
love and care first. "God has poured out his love into our
hearts by the Holy Spirit, whom he has given us" (Rom.
5:5). Love was modeled by the leaders of his church. He
lived and cared through their priesthood. The entire body
was linked to his shepherding care.

After this basic process, he could develop his church as
he planned. The first step needed to be established.

A healthy church will care about the members of that congregation and respond to their needs. A healthy church will
care about the turf, the place, the larger community where
God has called it to be. In the act of healing, a healthy
church will share its place with those in need. A healthy
church will have an identity that is carried in the rhythm
and pace of the congregation's life together. The identity
they share comes from God, who touches them as a people
in a place.[4]

4. Carl S. Dudley, *Making the Small Church Effective* (Nashville: Abingdon, 1978), pp. 119, 120.

A caring church becomes healthy. Christ's love finds in his people a prepared climate for his healing. It becomes the proper habitat for life by his Spirit to produce the health and wholeness of His love.

Christ's love through lay shepherds' care catalyzed his church. It became a healthy body ready to serve him in evangelism, teaching, further shepherding, and salting its community.

7

Satisfied Sheep and a Shepherd

Utopia had not arrived. The ultimate in a shepherding model was still to come off the assembly line at the Mission Hills Church. Nevertheless many of us involved in the emphasis believed we had something good.

There was progress with improvement. Benefits that extended to the congregation helped the senior pastor. There was greater contentment among the sheep of the congregation. Better pastoral care was provided to the individual sheep of the entire flock.

The senior pastor appeared not so burdened, more content and relaxed.

Satisfied Sheep

How can we measure the sense of well-being that care provided in the congregation? Like sheep in green pastures and beside still waters, it was there. There was a sense of security and intimate belonging, even though total membership increased each month.

A new member, arriving at church without knowing anyone, exemplified the satisfaction of many members. Charlotte Mather wrote:

Bob and Jan Burnside have shepherded me in a way I have never been helped before. I felt from the very first phone call that I had true friends in Christ. They extended a warmth of love just as God sends the warmth of sunshine. Just knowing that Bob and Jan are there is a "warm fuzzy." I thank God for directing me to Mission Hills where we have the Shepherding Groups.

Satisfaction varied in the lives of different members. These accomplishments were noteworthy.

The lay-shepherding teams enjoyed a meaningful service satisfaction. They were being used in a spiritual ministry that matters.

The spiritual nurturing care of human beings carries over into eternity. Scripture states that ministry is on Christ's behalf, in his stead. Many people on the lay-shepherding teams were involved previously in decision-making committees and boards. One deacon, executive of a large corporation, said:

I'm convinced that decision-making church boards are nongrowth situations. I've always been placed on them in every church where we've been members. They bring out my carnal nature. Sometimes I wonder what percentage of decisions I've helped make on church boards and committees through the years have mattered at all in eternity.

Some lay people have gifts and talents for ministry which supersede those of their pastors. They wait to be challenged in meaningful services for their Lord and eternity. Unfortunately, a high percentage of today's clergy discriminate against lay status rather than developing "tent makers."

Throughout the years of our history, have we made a serious mistake as we transferred so much pastoral care to "the man of the cloth"? What would be the effect if we should change our thinking to consider our ordained pastor as "training minister" and consider our laymen as "the real ministers"?[1]

In the lay-shepherding ministry I saw people take priesthood into their lives. They served, functioning as pastors in a distinguishing manner. The competency of lay persons in shepherding God's people far outshines the effectiveness of many professional ministers.

Lay shepherds reflected deep satisfaction in the nurturing, spiritual service.

Little Flock members expressed contentment because they were a cared-for people. Satisfaction of the sheep stems from two sources: the care of the lay shepherds and supporting friendship supplied by the Little Flock.

The care of the lay shepherds far exceeded the senior pastor's earlier expectations. I was grasping, looking for assistance to benefit my overextended situation. I didn't perceive that lay people could minister in a shepherding capacity to the extent they did. They extended comfort and encouragement to others whose troubles were similar.

One of the deacons was without employment for several months a few years ago. Each Wednesday morning he invited several men of the church who were without jobs as his guests at a restaurant. There at breakfast that deacon had a ministry of encouragement and prayer.

Telephone calls, notes, home visits, and prayers linked people to their lay shepherds. As the relationship blossomed the satisfaction swelled.

Several of the shepherding teams made "drop-in" calls to Little Flock members during the Christmas season. One deacon and deaconess delivered miniature poinsettia plants; another couple gave Christmas tree ornaments with Scripture on them; another brought small decorative holly plants to each household; others gave plates of Christmas

1. Charles W. Shedd. *The Pastoral Ministry of Church Officers* (Atlanta: John Knox Press, 1974), p. 15.

cookies and candies. Satisfaction, contentment, and reciprocal love resulted from such care.

The Little Flock was designed to be a small church family. At its best it functioned in this manner. When there
was illness, the Little Flock rallied to support and assist.
A member of the church was home as a terminal patient.
Church members took turns spending each night with the
patient.

During hospitalization and home recovery, the Little
Flock members assisted with food, transportation, lawn
cutting, snow shoveling, and child care.

The list of support and care was endless. The primary
contribution was not services rendered, which could be
bought. It was the friendship extended with assistance.
There was a satisfaction in belonging.

A young father of four small sons was hospitalized for
tests. Malignancy was feared. The concern and anxiety of
his little church family could have been no greater if there
were a close blood relationship.

The suburbs can be a very lonely place to live. Large
churches are often a collection of strangers. Such a community needs as someone has said, "the essential character of the small church, an intimacy, the capacity to know
and care about others."

A Sane Overseeing Shepherd

Compare the condition of the senior pastor, as he appeared initially, contrasted to this state in the epilogue.

Back in 1976 I was beginning to "want out" but was
hemmed in. My wife was happy in the church. Her un-
official role as assistant pastor in earlier years had dimin-
ished. The church had grown and acquired a multiple staff.

Church members gave every indication that they were
responding to my ministry and expecting a long pastorate.
Common sense indicated that closing my ministry would

be traumatic for the church, perhaps resulting in instability and loss.

I was tired inside. The joy of ministry was fading. Listed in my prayer book of those days, was the request: "Renew my call; give me a new vision of ministry."

At that moment I wanted release from the responsibility, which had become too much. I was convinced that I had activated the Peter Principle. I was inadequate to handle the situation of my own making. This overextended pastor would have welcomed a call to a less-demanding ministry.

A crisis was mounting. I needed to understand and apply the advice of Jethro to his son-in-law Moses.

> Moses' father-in-law replied. "What you are doing is not good. You and these people who come to you will only wear yourselves out. The work is too heavy for you; you cannot handle it alone. Listen now to me and I will give you some advice, and may God be with you. You must be the people's representative before God and bring their disputes to him. Teach them the decrees and laws, and show them the way to live and the duties they are to perform. But select capable men from all the people—men who fear God, trustworthy men who hate dishonest gain—and appoint them as officials over thousands, hundreds, fifties and tens. Have them serve as judges for the people at all times, but have them bring every difficult case to you; the simple cases they can decide themselves. That will make your load lighter, because they will share it with you. If you do this and God so commands, you will be able to stand the strain, and all these people will go home satisfied." (Exod. 18:17–23)

This Scripture portion projected a principle which renewed one pastor's life in the twentieth century. A modern-day Moses, of Denver, Colorado, can declare the wisdom of Jethro's counsel.

Sharing the task of shepherding with a corps of lay people brought sanity and satisfaction in several ways.

I multiplied myself into thirty-six other lives by sharing the responsibility of shepherding seven hundred people with them.

It wasn't as easy as it sounds. In the initial stages of planning the program and writing the training manual, plus preparing lessons for each week's session, I wondered if I had made a mistake.

Adding this expenditure of time and effort to an over-extended life appeared to be foolhardy. It was necessary to keep my long-range objective before me. At times of faltering, God's Spirit gave a clear vision of what it would be like "out there."

Several months into the program small encouragements came, but the possibility of a major shift did not occur until the second year. To my surprise, I had to decide again whether I really wanted to relinquish my exclusive rights to shepherding the body.

The real sharing and multiplying began when a part of myself was given up. My life merged with my lay-shepherd partners. Since then commendable and competent shepherding gives me deep personal satisfaction.

This is a higher quality than a sound investment of time and energy. My life is bound into the lives of those who share this ministry with me. I discovered my style of shepherding extending through them. Thirty-six people, trained, assigned, and committed to share shepherding made an impact superior to my one-man ministry of several years ago. It was no surprise that a corps of shepherds was producing more competent pastoral care than when it was under a one-man ministry. That knowledge enabled me to rest better nights. It lifted a considerable strain and stress from my daylight hours as well.

There was a special relationship between the lay shepherds and myself that I found most satisfying. They became my principal support group, even though I had a staff of six professionally trained people. The lay shepherds were my friends; an affinity existed in our lives. Our association, based on ministry and not decision making, resulted in a camaraderie that has been a zenith in my relational experiences.

This is in contrast to the feeling that prevailed between myself and my colleagues on our pastoral staff. While we had worked well together and have excellent rapport, because most of them were younger, I was the father figure or the "boss," even in the lighter, more social times.

The Chairman of the Board of Deacons met me early each Wednesday morning. We've laughed, cried, and prayed together. I've shared my deepest thoughts, greatest anxieties, and self-centered hurts with him. He has seen me at the throne room and under a juniper tree. This man was my friend, confidant, and partner. Other deacons with whom I've worked and shared through these years linked their lives with mine. They saw the best and worst side of their shepherding pastor. They accepted me anyway.

Many pastors speak of the pastorate as a lonely life, I do not. Partnership in the lay-shepherding ministry became my support group. Sanity and ministry satisfaction did not come in freeing up time for a magnitude of ministerial tasks. It came when sensing that personal gifts are tracking well. I realized that I will not be a superstar according to ministerial standards. I knew that the congregation needs a leader who as a man of God shepherds other shepherds.

The Lord reassigned me. I was promoted to a new job on the same ranch. He made a ranch foreman out of a shepherd.

8

Without a Head Shepherd?

This senior pastor had inner, conflicting loy-
alties at work in him. Remember that Jesus had said:

> I am the good Shepherd, the good Shepherd lays down his
> life for the sheep. The hired hand is not the shepherd who
> owns the sheep. So when he sees the wolf coming, he aban-
> dons the sheep and runs away. Then the wolf attacks the
> flock and scatters it. The man runs away because he is a
> hired hand and cares nothing for the sheep. (John 10:11–13)

After twelve years of ministry at the Mission Hills
Church; and with every outward reason to regard it as an
ideal setting in which to spend a lifetime of ministry, there
were interior signs of preparatory lift-off that only those
who have experienced it will fully understand.

This extended period of unrest was followed by a visit
and interview with the Emmanuel Baptist Church in
Mount Vernon, Washington. The need was incredible. For
years the Emmanuel Church had been one of the largest
and strongest evangelical churches between Seattle and
Vancouver, Canada. Several months prior to my first visit,
a major separation had spawned what was perceived as a
counterchurch or fellowship in the community.

The leadership of the flock left behind who visited with

me were still reeling from the impact of the loss of family
members and a lifetime of friends from their midst. The
wounding and hurt and desperate need for shepherding
care were heart gripping.

Back at the fold at Mission Hills there was the discovery
anew how much I loved the sheep there and the marvelous
corps of lay shepherds who had so willingly become co-
shepherds with me in the care of the congregation in
Denver.

If I were to leave the church, would it undergo a significant loss observed so frequently in the pastoral transition
of churches? Depict the scenario so commonplace, usually
in this order:

1. The pastor makes his decision to resign and accepts
   a call to another church. The congregation he has
   been serving as shepherd is unexpectant and unprepared for the announcement of his resignation. Those
   who have benefited the most from his ministry are
   devastated at his impending departure.
2. Once the decision has been made in the mind of the
   pastor and made public to the congregation, the pastor makes his mental move and begins to formulate
   his early days in his next ministry. His concluding
   ministry days begin a "lame-duck" phase.
3. To him the new church, yet unknown for its existing
   problems, has an aura of superiority to the church
   he is leaving. He embellishes the new church in his
   imagination and savors the days ahead. The two are
   unfairly compared to fortify and justify the rightness
   of his decision. His closing days become ones of a
   deepening disenchantment and disillusionment with
   the church he has served.
4. This is responded to by a portion of the congregation
   matching his mental leave taking. They, in a mental
   adjustment to the impending change in pastoral leadership, begin to notice the resigning pastor's weak-

nesses and flaws. They think, "He really wasn't as effective or as good a pastor as I thought. He is weak here; he let me down there. Perhaps the next minister will be stronger than he is, a better preacher of the Word, and a more caring shepherd."

5. A deterioration in quality of the relationship of the congregation and the resigning minister develops from the day of the resignation to the final farewell.

6. This erodes in a further slippage in the church following the exit of the pastor. At best the interim is a maintaining period; at its worst it becomes a mini-time of Judges, when everyone does that which is right in his sight. Because there is no permanent pastor, some of the congregation begin to visit other churches because they no longer feel a need to be faithful to the temporary supply in the pulpit of their own church. Attendance drops. Dissatisfaction rises in the congregation; discontent mounts. The Search Committee seems so secretive. A measure of mistrust and suspicion surfaces. As the interim lengthens, finances wane, and there is a loss of members. People seem unwilling to take on church responsibilities and ministries. Things grind to a halt. There is a wait-and-see-attitude everywhere.

7. This saga doesn't conclude the day the newly called minister arrives and starts his ministry. He discovers loss and a drifting and a state of deteriorated health in his new charge. The church needs strong leadership and immediately. Some in the congregation resist the change of leadership; others just do not personally care for the new pastor as they did the previous one; still others resent his necessary strong style of leadership in what should be a honeymoon period. So a loss and pulling away of some of the membership continues, even after the new minister arrives. He must begin the long, slow process of entering their lives and winning their hearts.

I had seen this script played out in numerous churches in the twelve years of ministry in Denver. I loved the Mission Hills flock. As a shepherd the thought of any possible loss was painful. A great amount of love and labor was wrapped up in the gathering and nurturing of that flock to its health and vitality. They could not be exposed to the attacks and scattering just described which are so common when a shepherd leaves his flock.

At that time of uncertainty I read John 10 and shuddered at the possible suggestion that in leaving I might be playing the role of "the hired hand." Within this context a mind change happened several times.

In company with this and in conflict with it was an increasing certainty that to close my heart and life to the need of the wounded church in Washington and a personal response to that need would be disobedience on my part. In spite of apprehension, there was solid knowledge that the Good Shepherd could be trusted with the flock in Denver if he were calling its present shepherd away.

Gently the preparation began. The lay shepherds were performing exemplary pastoral care. But without the head shepherd as catalyst and motivator there was a gnawing question of continuing effectiveness. The existing flock composition of minicross sections of the congregation at times seemed like artificial groupings. There had been some remarkable results as senior citizens were brought into the mainstream of the church and singles and single parents had a real family that included them. But the groupings didn't have a natural cohesiveness; there was no automatic flow without careful attention and a head shepherd's supervision. I knew that the system would flounder and possibly fail in my absence. A more natural flocking was needed for the interim, one that would provide a regular meeting of the lay shepherding team with their flock members, and one that would supply a spontaneous homogeneity.

The church was drawing over seven hundred people in

worship with twelve adult Sunday-school classes. Some of these were averaging more than fifty in attendance.

It was the time of year to reorganize the flocks and make assignments to new shepherding teams. With my encouragement and direction we decided to organize the Little Flocks according to the adult Sunday-school classes they attended or would attend if they chose to make Sunday school a part of their lifestyle. A list of all of the people of Mission Hills who did not attend adult Sunday-school classes was gathered. These included teachers of the Sunday school in other than adult classes and worshipers and members who were not Sunday-school attenders. These were contacted with the question: "If you were to attend an adult Sunday-school class which one would it be?" We explained that our question was simply for the purpose of putting households in Little Flocks for the coming year. With help and some explanation of teachers and approximate age groupings, everyone contacted made a choice.

From this compiled list of the adult Sunday-school attenders and prospects, we then assigned the appropriate number of shepherding teams to each adult class and selected class members and assigned them to Little Flock groupings of twelve to fifteen households under these respective shepherding teams.

The shepherding teams began to attend the adult Sunday-school classes that their flock members belonged to or had chosen as their class preference. They were able to observe absences of many of their flock members and in a very natural way contact them and function as watchful and caring shepherds. The smaller grouping of the adult Sunday-school class enabled the lay-shepherding team to have time before and after class to talk to various Little Flock members and begin to develop a growing relationship with them. Quite naturally these lay leaders began to function as class chaplains and assisted the teachers of their respective classes. In two adult classes that spring the deacons served in a dual capacity as teachers of the class and lay shepherds within the adult Sunday-school class structure. Regular Little Flock activities with their assigned deacon/deaconess team separated from the rest of the adult Sunday-school class for the smaller group functions.

This more natural flow of relationships and shepherding team ministries to the Little Flocks within the Sunday-school context was immediately apparent. There was a spontaneous homogeneity to each newly formed flock. Most of the members of each Little Flock were generally acquainted with each other. Some were good friends. There were numerous side benefits. The lay-shepherding teams contacted absentee class members who were in their Little Flocks. The commitment of worship attenders to a Sunday-school class choice made them prospects for that class. A surprising increase in the average Sunday-school attendance was evident.

It was in such a natural arrangement of flocking that the need for a head shepherd's role of stimulating to ministry was reduced.

The disadvantage was that the Little Flocks no longer represented a cross section of the congregation. The elderly were isolated again from the mainstream of the church because their adult Sunday-school class was confined to their age bracket. The singles experienced a similar disadvantage. Single parents and their children no longer found a support group they could identify with representing father and grandfather images.

Under the new flocking arrangement each of the nineteen Little Flocks were assigned a shut-in and/or an elderly person as a special ministry project. Care and gestures of attention and concern began to flow to previously neglected shut-ins. This distribution of the elderly among the Little Flocks enabled younger active flock members to share the responsibility to bereaved families at funeral dinners and the provision of food to homes in times of crisis.

Care of the sheep was ably being performed without my

involvement. These rearrangements were made in the months prior to my resignation and as the probability of my leaving the Mission Hills Church became increasingly evident to me.

The shepherds and the sheep were assigned and in place. This ranch foreman was about to be transferred to another ranch thousands of miles away. For a while they would all be without a human head shepherd. How would they fare?

9

When the Shepherd Leaves . . .

My wife and I flew to Mount Vernon for the candidating weekend unknown to the congregation of the Mission Hills church. The Moderator and the Chairman of the Shepherding Board had been aware from near the beginning of negotiations because they were my prayer partners and confidants. The pastoral staff and the secretaries were aware of the impending weekend and its possible significance.

That weekend in Washington state fortified and confirmed our earlier impressions and suspicions. The Emmanuel Church was in an extremely unhealthy condition. The network of buildings and the developed church campus would make most churches envious of such a facility. But the split/separation was only four months old. This once strong, proud church had undergone an amputation, and it was still reeling and bleeding from the shock. The people were like the rejected spouse in a divorce action and going through the subsequent stages of grief. They no longer knew who they were, or who was with them, nor certain who had left their fellowship, and the church certainly didn't know where it was going.

The Emmanuel Church needed a shepherd and a leader

immediately. The newly formed fellowship was active in recruiting the fringe elements of those who remained at Emmanuel and it was gaining new recruits weekly.

I was gripped with compassion akin to that of Jesus:

When he saw the crowds he had compassion on them, because they were harassed and helpless, like sheep without a shepherd (Matt. 9:36).

My wife was the reluctant follower as we began that weekend of exploration that could change our lives. She did not want to leave twelve years of friends, an ideal church situation, a home full of memories, an affirming job, two married daughters, and four grandchildren. As the weekend progressed she found herself at about every turn ministering to many hurting, emotionally wounded, grieving women on that so called candidating weekend. The devastation of a church of people gripped the two of us.

How do you tell a congregation that you are leaving them as their shepherd? There was an element of the emotional guilt of betrayal in the consideration. The potential for reactions of disappointment and rejection loomed imminent on the scene. I was their spiritual shepherd. They were my sheep and lambs. Their present shepherd had seen them spiritually born, baptized, discipled, nurtured, married, and becoming parents. In the process they had become a part of my life and my life was interwoven with theirs.

I fluctuated subjectively between my desire to slip out of town unnoticed and play my farewell and the culmination of a successful ministry to the hilt for personal glory and gratification.

In the resigning process, too many ministers without advance signal or forewarning of any kind on a given Sunday at the close of a message read their resignation as pastor in a rather cavalier manner to the shock, dismay, and unbelief of unexpecting parishioners. Such a scene is not unlike the reaction of a mate who one day without any advance notice hears his spouse say to him: "I'm leaving you. I'm filing for divorce. This is good-bye."

Leadership in 1983 interviewed Ray Oswald regarding the "Pastor's Passages."

> The interviewers asked: "You mentioned . . . moving from one parish to another. What are the important elements here?"
>
> Oswald: "Learning to say goodbye. Our research on termination styles of clergy shows they are typically bad, not allowing opportunity for people to express their feelings, to say what this pastor has meant. Maybe pastors feel it's maudlin. Usually, however, they slip off into the night without really saying good-bye, and that can undercut everything they've done up till then. People can question whether the pastor really cared for them at all."[1]

How does a shepherd leave when God calls him to lead another flock? Is there a proper way to effect the change and maintain a loving relationship between the two and minimize emotional estrangement with its resulting ill-health?

Ours, pastor and people, had been an open and honest relationship. Never was there a time when I needed the prayers of the people I'd loved and served as I did during that pivotal period.

Two decisions made at this juncture in ministry were very helpful to all of us. First, there was the determination not to make a final decision regarding the call that was extended to me by the Emmanuel Church for a two-week period, and I told them that. Second, I decided to be as candid and open and aboveboard with everyone as I could possibly be in the choice to go or remain.

The saga of those two weeks follows:

1. "The Pastor's Passages," an interview with Ray Oswald, *Leadership*, Vol. IV, Number 4, Fall, 1983.

1. *June 15, 1982* Tuesday morning after returning from
   the weekend in Mount Vernon, Washington, I shared
   with the church secretaries and bookkeeper my
   impressions of the weekend and walked through the
   entire saga step-by-step and answered any questions
   they had.

   I repeated this at the pastoral staff meeting that
   afternoon. All of the associate pastors, assistants, and
   interns were present. I described the devastated condition of the Emmanuel Church. The staff asked
   questions on the subject: "If you as senior pastor
   were to leave . . . what would happen?" We talked
   both scenarios through in detail.

2. *June 16, 1982* Wednesday morning at 7:00 A.M. I met
   in my office with Bill Ward, the moderator-elect and
   the man who as chairman of the Deacon Board for
   two years had been my partner in the lay-shepherding
   ministries at Mission Hills. As my prayer partner he
   had known the possibility and prospect of the Emmanuel Church almost as soon as it became a serious consideration. Bill was more than mildly involved
   in that decision. If I were to leave, the leadership of
   the church would be his during the interim. Again
   I opened my heart to him. As an astute businessman
   and a wise spiritual person he asked many discerning
   questions.

3. *June 17, 1982* Thursday evening a special shepherding board meeting was called at Bill and Sharon Ward's
   home. All of the lay-shepherding teams but two were
   present. None knew the purpose of the meeting. It
   was an emotionally charged gathering as I recounted
   my restlessness of recent months and then the brief
   history and grim description of the Emmanuel
   Church. I walked them through the previous weekend in detail and gave brief vignettes of impressions
   from my wife's perspective and my own. Some of
   these varied.

It was the most difficult task of those two weeks. They
were my partners in the pastoral ministry of the church.
Together we had hammered out the lay-shepherding ministry from scratch.

There was one young deaconess whom I had spiritually
steered through singleness into engagement, and then
married to the young man who sat beside her, and dedicated their two children. I had been the only pastor she'd
ever known. She said, "Pastor, if we weren't so healthy, if
we were a hurting church, too, would you stay?"

We cried and prayed together that night, and I knew that
I was loved and trusted. If I left, they would believe God
had called and led me. There was certain knowledge they
would not harbor the thought I was betraying them.

How could the drive home that evening be described?
Mine was a free and uplifted spirit. I was not a hireling.
And he was the shepherd of the church. It was his. And I
was his—free to move at his command. The people I had
come to love the most had said in so many ways they
trusted me and unknowingly they had released me. In
retrospect, there was the knowledge that night I would be
leaving.

4. *June 18, 1982* Friday I composed a letter to the entire congregation. This written communication in
   candid and honest terms described as succinctly as
   possible the Emmanuel Church in Mount Vernon,
   their crisis, our visit to the church, and impressions.
   The letter was interlaced with love and appreciation
   for the people of the Mission Hills Church. The closure of the letter was a call to prayer for a decision
   that would be made in the next two weeks.
   I concluded the letter with these words:

You are my people and the sheep of a pasture the Lord has
entrusted to my care. We all need his guidance in decisions
that need to be made in the near future.

I love you and realize that there are few pastors privileged
to write this sort of candid letter to his congregation with
the knowledge that whichever way the Lord leads there will
be a bond of reciprocal love and support.

Let's pray together. . . .
(signed) Pastor CHUCK
C. VER STRATEN

This significant communique was prepared for mailing
by my personal secretary to be mailed on Saturday with
projected receipt of it on Monday or Tuesday.

In reflection, this written communication was a master
stroke in preparing people and including them in the final
phases of the decision-making procedure. That personal
message received in the privacy of homes and read there
enabled everyone to know what was happening and to be
included in the process.

5. *June 19, 1982* Saturday morning at 8:00 A.M. at the
   fireplace in the fellowship room twelve to fifteen
   men had gathered for several years to share and pray.
   There was an intimacy between us that was the finest community I've ever experienced and that level
   of relationship has not been duplicated again. On
   this eventful morning I not only verbally took them
   step-by-step through the entire process and where I
   was in the decision, which was inclining toward a
   lift-off, but I disclosed my fears and personal needs.
   They participated in my life that morning and there
   was some very wise counsel. And on our knees there
   was prayer for an extended period of time.
6. *June 20, 1982* Sunday: No reference was made in a
   public way. Private encounters were personally sup-
   portive. Several were aggressive dissuaders. Some of
   this continued through the week as the letter of communication was received by the congregation and
   widespread conversation occurred within the body.

7. *June 25, 1982* Early Friday morning I was awakened and went to the family room for prayer. There in a classic encounter with the Lord, the Macedonian call to Skagit Valley in the Northwest came. An inner assurance/knowledge was born. I knew that I was leaving from and going to what he had prepared. The decision had been made.

8. *June 26, 1982* Saturday at 8:00 A.M. I told the support group of praying partners that I would be resigning the following day at the close of the service. Prayer was directed for that moment. I disclosed this projected agenda to every one who asked that Saturday and before the service on Sunday.

9. *June 27, 1982* Sunday: The brief sermon was on "Discovering the Will of God." It was an attentive audience. After a brief, concluding prayer, I stepped down to the communion table and said that there were personal words I needed to express.

I thanked them for their prayers, and the love, care, and counsel that had been given to my wife and me the previous week. There were words of affirmation and love and some semihyperbolic statements were made. It was a sentimental moment.

Then I read the statement of resignation which was full and warm with emphasis on my certainty of God's call and my submission to him. It was obviously a poor choice from limited human perspective. I voiced that. And it was true. The resignation was concluded with the words of Jeremiah 29:11, " 'For I know the plans I have for you,' declares the LORD, 'plans to prosper you and not to harm you, plans to give you hope and a future.' "

After I placed the resignation on the communion table I verbalized the question I perceived was uppermost in their minds: "So what happens now?" Then with elaboration I walked through the scary scenario that I described in the previous chapter. The details of the disaffection commonly developing in closure of ministry and the lame-duck syndrome were disclosed with embellishments enough to make them very real.

Next there was the depiction of the too-typical interim period between pastors. Graphically I described the diso-rientation and chaos that frequently immobilized congre-gations in the interim desert of leaderlessness. I spared nothing in portraying the inclination of members to be-come absentees or use the unaccountable period to visit other churches.

There was the resulting finale of this potential saga de-picted in a weakened church and the subsequent unheal-thy climate produced by chaos, and dissensions and the slippage of membership. The loss of several years of pre-vious ministry gone down the drain as the new pastor comes to a weakened and wounded vessel to again make "ship shape" and provide leadership to its helm.

Then with assurance that came from God's Spirit and as some said later, "an anointing from him," I said:

> But that does not need to happen here. To my knowledge this church is in amazing good health. I know of no major problems. If you do, don't share it right now. If ignorance is bliss, let me be blissful.

> There is a deep respect and affection between the senior pastor and the people of this church. I am not leaving for any reason. If it were my preference, I would like to spend the rest of my ministering days in your midst. God has a great future planned for this church.

> Because of these circumstances and relationships we have the opportunity to demonstrate how to handle a transition between pastors. The success of this church in building a model of a bridge between pastors and discovering God's man for the next era of its pilgrimage will provide a tre-mendous encouragement to other churches when they face a pastoral change. Some of the horror stories they have heard can be matched with hope and confidence without fear by the Mission Hills story.

I plead with you, I require of you, don't pull back. Don't you dare begin to visit other churches in the period to come. Be more faithful in attendance than you have been in the past. As Scripture says, "Let us not give up meeting together ... but let us encourage one another ..." (Heb. 10:25).

A further word: I have no intention of becoming a lame-duck pastor. We've worked too hard together in this ministry to bring this church to its present health and vitality to let three or four years of fruitful labor go down the drain during the interim period. I am not moving mentally until the day the moving van arrives. I will work with the leadership of the church and the lay shepherds to prepare you to move through the era of change with flying colors. I will spend the time necessary to prepare the pastoral staff to function without a senior pastor.

The Executive Board of the church has already indicated their desire and interest in an interim preacher for filling this pulpit on a regular and consistent basis during the interim. They want one voice and not a series of pulpit suppliers. I will assist them as needed so this interim pulpit placement will be secured before I leave. I will encourage the selection of a Search Committee for the new senior pastor by the executive board immediately. If that Search Committee desires it, I will meet with them and give counsel in the development of a church profile for use in the search. The very best of materials sent by churches to me through the years with the best letters of inquiry I have received will be given to them for study and models.

And most important, I will pray with a fervent heart daily and regularly for you as a church and for the man God is preparing as shepherd for this place and this pulpit. These prayers will continue until the day the new shepherd stands in this pulpit as your pastor. I will be available to Bill Ward, the new moderator of the church. He will become the head and leader of this church in the months to come.

We believe that God is sovereign. He causes all things to work together for good. He has here at Mission Hills an excellent instrument to use as a model to demonstrate that Jesus Christ is Lord here. He is in control. Jesus is the Shepherd and leader of this body.

The sovereign Lord of his church everywhere has chosen you to demonstrate to the church world how to handle a pastoral transition. My word to you is to "pull it off well." I like your style and I love you. Let's pray.

The response was amazing. The congregation had just moved into a new era of faith. God anointed that moment to launch them on a mission. The words I spoke were timely and wise, but there was another dynamic present that catalyzed the situation and propelled it upward.

If there was a sliver of motivation to orchestrate for a tearful response and reaction to my resignation, a flood of "oh, nos," it wasn't pulled off that day. There was sufficient love expressed to warm a pastor's heart, but there was foremost a sense of destiny and future and resolve to beat the odds. An esprit de corps had caught the congregation. They were going to share in a model that would demonstrate how to carry off a pastoral transition well. They were already on mission. I knew they were ready.

The two remaining months were among the most active of my ministry in that church. My counsel was freely sought on all sides.

Leadership's interview with Ray Oswald highlighted the need for time in a proper closure.

Question: How long should you be a lame duck?
OSWALD: Closure takes a minimum of two or three months. In one sense, you are a lame duck but that's good. You can stop programming and bolstering your favorite activities. Your task now is closure, and that takes time, especially if you're well liked. People's initial reaction is shock and denial. They can't say good-bye on the spot. There's a subtle withdrawal and they come back. This can't be done in two weeks.

Good closure prevents lots of problems. Pastors don't re-alize that in order to start well in a new parish they must say good-bye to the old parish. . . . If you close well, you can get on with life, put to rest one chapter, and begin another. Both congregation and clergy feel better about themselves, and they can reach out to the new minister without emotional scars.[2]

Roles were defined and responsibility and accountabil-ity were spelled out and referred to time and again. Ref-erence to these in the pulpit and at board and committee meetings and the weekly church mailout clarified and crystallized who was who for everyone's understanding.

The newly elected moderator, Bill Ward, was the leader, the acting head of the church. Two years as chairman of the shepherding boards and prayer partner and confidant of the senior pastor had prepared him. The Rev. George Loring, associate of Christian Education and Administra-tion, was to function as the administrator of the church, leader of the pastoral staff and as the ordained minister of the church, performing the weddings and funerals and other ministries expected of an ordained clergyman. Additional staff was secured for the interim:

1. Dr. James Means of the Homiletics Department of Denver Seminary was secured as the interim preacher. This was arranged and announced several weeks prior to the resigning pastor's last Sunday. His fine ser-mons were a key factor in the consistency in atten-dance during the interim.
2. Additional staff were added. a. a full-time interim youth pastor; b. the minister of music was added full time to the staff; c. a part-time director of children's ministry proved key in releasing Rev. Loring to func-tion in full administration and pastoral capacities.

2. *Ibid* p. 14.

3. The Search Committee for the new senior pastor was selected and organized and had begun to meet a month prior to the conclusion of my ministry. The composition as well as the chairmanship of that committee was undoubtedly designed in heaven. They experienced a remarkable community in the days of their search and because of this quality were able to function fully by consensus.

> When I am the designated leader I have found that once a group becomes a community, my nominal job is over. . . . Its decisions are reached by consensus. Communities have sometimes been referred to as leaderless groups. It is more accurate, however, to say that a community is a group of all leaders.[3]

The Senior Pastor Search Committee invited me to meet with them prior to leaving. Many questions were asked to gain insight into the initiation of the candidating process as seen from the pastor's perspective. The importance of developing and producing a thorough and attractive church profile was emphasized. Several of the best which had been sent to me through the years were given to them to use as models. The committee eventually produced the finest profile of a church I've examined. There was some instruction regarding the writing of inquiry letters and samples of these, good and bad, were left with the committee.

The closing period of the gathering evolved into a very heart-to-heart hour that would warm any pastor's heart in reflection. I was their spiritual mentor of many years and the trust level between all of us was at summit-level dimensions.

The last Sunday in August concluded twelve and one-half years of significant ministry. The classic joys and sorrows of leave taking interlaced that day. Household items

3. M. Scott Peck, *The Different Drum: Community Making and Peace* (New York: Simon and Schuster, 1987), p. 72.

were packed. The moving van was scheduled to arrive early the next morning. The family, two daughters, sons-in-law, and four grandchildren were very solemn and tear-ful. My wife was already moving from one stage of grief to another, and I was stiff-lipped and obedient.

The Mission Hills interim saga was just beginning. Worship service maintained its previous attendance average throughout the interim. The preaching of Dr. Means was well received. His homiletic flair attracted some new people. The laity moved into action. Reports of new creative programming for the interim era were exciting. The church was obviously "on mission." A public-school teacher was added to the staff as part-time children's director. New life and movement was injected into a vacuum of the church that needed leadership. The lay-shepherding teams became pastors and chaplains in the adult classes. Their weekly contacts on absentees and the assimilation of new people in the classes into their Little Flocks caused adult attendance to soar. Because they brought their youth and children, the entire Sunday school attendance was considerably higher than the previous year.

Excitement and enthusiasm surfaced throughout the church. The model was performing far better than projected.

In March, six months into the interim period, the Rev. George Loring, the pastoral staff person who functioned as the church administrator, in a letter evaluating my preparing the Mission Hills church for the interim wrote: "I continue to be amazed with what God is doing and how he is accomplishing certain things." Loring listed things that were done properly by the resigning senior pastor which helped the people of Mission Hills accept the resignation and prepare them for the transition.

1. He informed the key leadership of his thinking and his possible resignation.
2. He sent a personal letter to the total membership

communicating to them his thinking and possible resignation.

3. After his announcement of resignation, there were a number of key things that were done to insure stability during the interim. There was the securing of additional staff to help provide guidance in the transition: a. an interim preacher; b. a full-time interim youth pastor (the associate pastor of youth resigned several months before the senior pastor's resignation); c. the adding of the minister of music to the staff full time; d. the later addition of a part time children's director.

4. There was a unanimity among the added staff of their commitment to the church during the interim.

5. There was a commitment by the various lay leaders to the interim period and working to make it work.

6. The key item that prepared the church to function in health during the interim was a strong sense of leadership ability in the staff and the leadership boards of the church.

Loring continued in his assessment of the church after being without a senior pastor for over six months:

Attendance is up over the previous year in the Sunday school. The church has not dwindled. People are still being saved, baptized, and added to the church. There is consistency and continuity in the worship services. The church realizes its focus and its emphasis. There is an attitude that things are happening and continue to happen in spite of the fact that we are without a senior pastor. I cannot think of any items that could have been done to better equip the church. Life has continued as planned.

In the late spring the Mission Hills Senior Pastor Search Committee with complete unanimity found the man they wanted to present to the church, the Rev. Clyde Mc-

Dowell, associate pastor of the Wooddale Baptist Church in the Minneapolis, Minnesota, vicinity.

In late June during a brief visit in Denver, Bill Trollinger, Search Committee Chairman, invited me to his home and to lunch. With considerable excitement he highlighted the search, gave me McDowell's resume which we read together, and then we listened to the tape of a sermon by Clyde McDowell.

We rejoiced in God's selection. We worshiped our sovereign Lord together in a sense of awe at his goodness.

Clyde McDowell was scheduled for the rigorous traditional candidating weekend at Mission Hills. The preceding week I finally located him by telephone at his father's in South Carolina. We talked very briefly and then I said, "Clyde, Bill showed me your resume and I listened to the tape of a sermon of yours, and I'm excited about the prospect of your being the next pastor at Mission Hills. I want to have prayer on the phone with you about your candidating there this weekend."

During the prayer a dynamic connection of ministries occurred. We have spoken several times since of the significance of that moment for both of us.

Five years have rushed by since McDowell became the senior pastor of the Mission Hills church. He is in the Olympic Class as a senior minister. Because he is a secure person, confident of the direction in which he wants to shepherd the church, it was not necessary to belittle or replace the foundations of the previous ministry. He maximized those foundations and built on them and the church membership wholly followed his leadership. My son-in-law and daughter are active members of the church and Pastor Clyde is the pastor of four of our grandchildren.

The Mission Hills Baptist Church is in the process of building a new thirteen-hundred-seat sanctuary. The *Rocky Mountain News*, one of Denver's two major newspapers, recently featured the church in a front-page spread: "Baby Boomers Return to Church." Mission Hills is on its way to becoming a great church. It has provided not just a model for pastoral transitions; its record demonstrates a church orchestrated by the leadership of the Holy Spirit.

10

Shepherding Care
Heals a Wounded Church

Skagit Valley, located halfway between Seattle, Washington, and Vancouver, British Columbia, is one of those incredibly beautiful places on earth. The upper reaches of the Valley sweep east upward to the Northern Cascades thirty-five to forty miles and empties westward in the Puget Sound amidst the parting of the San Juan Islands. The alluvial soil of the flat valley is reported to be the richest and deepest anywhere outside the Nile Valley itself. Dairy farms, vegetable crops, and bulb growing abound. More tulips are grown in this green valley than anywhere with the exception of Holland.

A local author has penned words to describe the Skagit Valley:

She spreads her green cloak from the rugged Cascade peaks to the seashores of the San Juans. Beneath her hem, pearly oyster and sweet clams gather close. She trims her skirts with rich farmland, fields of yellow tulips and the greens of broccoli and spinach. Crisp carrots, purple cabbages, and apple blossoms weave a tapestry with golden fields of grain. Salmon thread her rivers as she buttons herself with true blue berries and those of richest red, while Bessie pours the milk and cream.[1]

The hub of the valley is its county seat, Mount Vernon, an elite town/city of sixteen thousand population. The immediate environment boasts forty thousand people. The main artery through the new business district of the town goes right past Skagit Community College and the seven acres of sprawling and impressive buildings known as the Emmanuel Baptist Church.

This well-known church in the Northwest had a significant ministry for decades and had established its reputation as a strong lighthouse between Seattle and Vancouver since the fifties.

Six months after the resignation of its long-term senior pastor, nearly a third of the families of the Emmanuel congregation signed a letter of separation. It was worded in the most positive of Christian terms.

We, the undersigned, believing that God is leading us in the formation of a new fellowship in the area, and in the spirit of cooperation and noninvolvement in the internal affairs of the Emmanuel Baptist Church, request that our names be placed on the inactive membership list of Emmanuel. It is our constant desire to maintain strong bonds of love, friendship, and cooperation that continue to unite us as brothers and sisters in our Lord Jesus Christ.

This statement of intent was read in the morning worship, February 7, 1982. The following Sunday a large group of people met in a rented facility, and the Emmanuel body that remained were reminded of the separation and church division by half-filled pews, emptiness, and loneliness.

Two weeks after the devastating day in which that statement was read in the church service and a prayer was made

1. Julie Wilkerson Rousseau, *Alice Bay Cookbook* (Mount Vernon: Quartsize Books, 1985), p. 1.

for those leaving, the associate pastor of the Emmanuel Church, who was the acting interim minister, resigned to become the recognized leader of the newly formed fellowship.

Those leaving had a great sense of relief; a remarkable esprit de corps accompanied them. They were "on a roll" and assembled in a series of several temporary meeting places. Other dissatisfied Christians from different churches joined them. The week-by-week drift and shift from the Emmanuel Church continued. Disparagingly some spoke of the big empty barn up on College Way. Someone later observed that many of the more "progressive types" left the Emmanuel Church in the first and second waves of departees.

This was the valley and these were the people where God called us to shepherd to healing and restoration in the fall of 1982. The next three years were to be the most difficult and trying of our entire ministry.

The various stages of grief were written all over the lives and emotions of those who were left behind in the Emmanuel Church. Hours were spent in counseling. Every home visit required listening to each individual tell his account of what had happened to cause the separation from their particular perspective. Some were still in the shock and denial stages of grief. Many people at this point in time were dealing with anger and its varied ramifications. Bitterness abounded. I looked for some wholeness, some health—and found almost none.

Almost immediately I realized that a strict partisan approach—siding subjectively with the remaining members—would be unwise. A significant number who remained at Emmanuel shared some of the sentiments of those who left.

An extended luncheon meeting with the former associate pastor and an intimate prayer time in a car defused a growing suspicion of evil intent or design on his part. That meeting reinforced my earlier hypothesis of his responsibility being caused by naivety and lack of discerning judgment.

In those early days of ministry my leadership was needed in helping the remaining congregation understand and interpret the causes and effects of the church divorce that had so affected their lives. It seemed wise to listen and draw the hurting out so they could verbalize their understanding and interpretation of what had happened. This was a long process.

I confess that it was aided by a curiosity. What causes a church split? What factors move a large congregation of people to a point of fomented anger and dissension to a level where separation seems the only solution? As I ministered to lives that had been emotionally damaged because of that particular church split, there was a growing anger toward the proliferation of church division in general. It seemed to parallel the increase of marital dissolutions nationwide.

So I experienced increasing antipathy toward any church division. As God hates marital divorce, there was a growing conviction that he hates divorce within his body. The shepherd heart placed within me was constrained to gather the flock of God, to lead them beside still waters and in green pastures and to heal them.

These instincts were repulsed with the wounding and scattering that occurs in most flock separations and church splits.

More and more I suspect that most church divisions are caused by the unseen false shepherd who lies to lead God's people into paths where the true Shepherd would never lead them.

It became immediately evident that the Emmanuel Church as a whole was still in a stage of denial in our first weeks of ministry. In spite of the request of the departing families to be placed on an inactive status of membership (and many others were retained on the membership rolls who should have been removed several years previously), the Board of Deacons found dealing with this matter extremely painful. After a personal contact with each family no longer attending had been made, and the request of many that their names be removed, the final vote to do so was with the greatest reluctance. One of the warm-hearted deacons just before voting declared: "I want to abstain, but I cannot. It's what they want. It's one of the hardest things I've ever done."

Shepherding was needed to help them discover what had happened, why it had happened, and begin to assist them in interpreting whether it was right or wrong. How were they to feel about all of this and how could each express his personal feelings?

John Wallace in *Control in Conflict* has observed:

When conflict arises, a major hindrance is the reluctance to admit a problem. Too often our attitude is "Just don't discuss it, it'll go away." Sometimes I'm tempted to heed advice given me when I was a rural pastor. A farmer counselled me about discord in our church. "Preacher, just walk around it, step over it, don't try to move it, and you won't stir up any stink." Such advice sometimes leaves unpleasant consequences, both in the church and barnyard.[2]

In order to effect full healing to the Emmanuel Church it was necessary to discover and understand the factors that came together to cause separation and the resultant rupture in relationships.

We nursed the wounded and began to minister in a community where unprovoked hostilities were encountered that could be traced only to residual effects of the separation. The full story requires another book and is not entirely germane to how shepherding healed a wounded church.

The chairman of the Board of Deacons, Don Sicklesteel,

2. John Wallace, *Control in Conflict* (Nashville: Broadman Press, 1982), p. 16.

had already mobilized the deacons during the interim between the division and my installation as senior pastor in a calling program on watch-care lists. He had ordered enough *The Deacon Family Ministry Plan Resource Books* to begin a training program using that book.[3]

The watch-care deacons were engaged in a visitation in the homes during that critical period. The framework was already established for the inception of a lay-shepherding ministry.

During the interviewing phase of my contact with the Emmanuel Church the deacons of the church were the group that most attracted me. They gave every evidence of desiring personal growth and wanting to be used. I saw prime timber for the building of an effective lay ministry. Don, the chairman, impressed me as a person of faith with a great desire to be nurtured and discipled. He became the primary building block in the first stage of the healing process. This head deacon was like a sponge to receive any spiritual nurture I gave. Our Saturday evening prayer together was the highlight of each of our weeks.

Almost immediately efforts were made to incorporate the wives of the deacons into their husband's ministries. Unlike the Mission Hills Church, the duties of the official Board of Deaconesses were established and did not include shepherding; few of the deacons' wives were elected to that board.

The training at Emmanuel was less intense than that given in Denver. The beginning phase of the lay-shepherding training was given two nights a month. A half-hour's training was given at the regular meeting and a full hour, using much of the previous material, was presented at a second monthly meeting.

The wives did not participate in the beginning phase of

3. Charles F. Treadway, *The Deacon Family Ministry Plan Resource Book* (Nashville: Convention Press, 1979).

the training. At overnight retreats they received intensi-
fied instruction.

There were several reasons for initiating the ministry of
lay shepherding at a slower pace than was done in the
previous church.

1. *I was overwhelmed immediately with the vast
   counseling of scores of hurting people.* And I was
   trying to piece together the puzzle of what had happened, its causes, and how to help the congregation
   understand and interpret it.
2. *The church for decades had been dominated by a
   fortress mentality.* They were the largest church in
   the vicinity. There was no history of cooperation with
   other churches. The community viewed the Emmanuel Church as isolationist. Combined with this, it
   was a church that was generally geared to a spectator
   mentality. The primary focus had been on the platform, music, and preaching, with a high appreciation
   for performance.

   I was interested in shepherding the church in the
   direction of outreach and changing its primary focus
   to a participative, caring ministry to the body. To
   redirect the Emmanuel Church required active
   teaching and leadership at all levels that challenged
   every skill and ability that could be mustered. The
   encouraging thing was that on every side the people
   of Emmanuel and its leadership were ready to become the people and the church God wanted them
   to be if they could discover what that was. Their
   response sent me to the Word and to my knees. With
   the passing of time there was a growing conviction
   that Christ was going to rebuild his church.
3. *A third reason for initiating the ministry of lay shepherding at a slower pace had organizational history.*

   The organizational structure of the church was a
   maze. The deacons were perceived to be the leading

board of the church. They had been blamed by those leaving the church as indecisive and ineffectual. The constitution however, named the Church Board, consisting of all the officers of the church—nearly forty persons—as the top decision-making board of the church. In truth at best it was a ratifying board. In reality each of the six major boards and committees did what they wanted to. There was much overlap and very little accountability.

Reorganization eventually established an executive council made up of the chairpersons of the major boards and the moderator. Nurturing and retraining and reeducating the congregation to view the deacons as lay pastors and the spiritual leaders, not the decision makers, required a two-to-three-year period.

The concept of Little Flocks was received readily by the congregation. The wives of the deacons were very cooperative in planning Little Flock functions and the social and care life of the church soon revolved around the Little Flock ministry. Perhaps the fragmentation and resulting need for identification with a small group worked in favor of the small groupings. The Fellowship Halls were reserved well in advance for shared buffets and Little Flock gatherings of all manner of activities. Home gatherings were well attended in the smaller community of a lifetime of friends.

Love began to flow as care and compassion touched the body through caring shepherds and caring people.

An unknown entity of people who called themselves "Encouragement Incorporated" began a ministry in secret. People perceived to need a lift would suddenly find in their offices or on their doorsteps carmel popcorn in ribbon-decorated coffee cans with an enclosed note of affirmation and encouragement, signed ENCOURAGEMENT, INC.

When people shared openly in gatherings or brought life-sharing testimonies, the phantomlike angels in our midst would strike again. To this day even I am uncertain as to who these individuals were. But Encouragement, Inc. left a stir and uplifted spirits wherever they touched down.

Notes and letters of love and encouragement flowed from household to household in a fashion I've never seen in another church. Thoughtfully selected gifts, many hand-made or home-cooked, enhanced special relationships.

The focus of the church changed from the platform and the preacher and the music ministry of the church to each other. (Hopefully the former did not suffer too much in the process of changed perspective!) Through Christ's shepherding care and his representative servant/leaders Emmanuel became a caring church.

The deacons met for an overnight retreat in a San Juan Island home the third year. In discovering Emmanuel's identity or identifying the reason for the changes that were occurring in our midst, it was determined that our time apart from fellowship would be to hammer out a one-sen-tence purpose statement for the Emmanuel Church. Gene Sampley, the new chairman of the Board of Deacons was by vocation the Director of Public Works of Skagit County. He was thoroughly trained in management by objective principles. It was laborious effort for the seventeen men as they sought to refine a statement expressing the church's reason for being. Again and again it was necessary to re-learn the difference between procedure and purpose, duties and mission, goals and objectives. I'm certain that most of the men, as they settled in their sleeping bags Friday night, felt frustrated and thought the effort was a waste of time. One word kept coming to ascendancy that evening as the lay shepherds kept coming back to the end result, the mission of the church and their own ministries. That word was *maturity*. We slept on our frustrations and questioned the value of the venture.

In the devotional time the next morning, one of the deacons, Rich Cornwell, shared the Scripture God had di-rected him to in his quiet time by the sea.

Ephesians 4:11–13: It was he [Christ] who gave some to be apostles, some to be prophets, some to be evangelists, and some to be pastors and teachers, to prepare God's people for works of service, *so that* the body of Christ may be built up until we all reach unity in the faith and in the knowledge of the Son of God and *become mature,* attaining to the whole measure of the fullness of Christ (italics added).

With that text and its "so that" (purpose and direction) the lay shepherds with their chairman's astute leadership worked out a simple purpose statement: "To bring people to maturity in Christ."

We had no idea how that would change our shepherding ministries or the direction and identity of the entire Emmanuel Church.

The lay shepherds now knew what they wanted for the people in their Little Flocks. Their earnest desire and prayer was that their flock members would be brought to maturity in Christ. Their earnest prayers were the same as the Holy Spirit's ministry in them.

2 Corinthians 3:18: And we . . . are being transformed into his likeness with ever-increasing glory, which comes from the LORD, who is the Spirit.

My preaching and teaching ministry had a direction it did not have before.

For the pastor-supervisor to supervise, he must have a healthy . . . and correct understanding of the purpose and function of the church. If he does not know what the church should be about, he will not know if and when they are about their father's business.[4]

4. Benjamin S. Baker, *Shepherding the Sheep* (Nashville: Broadman Press, 1983), p. 24.

All of the organizations and ministries of the church began to evaluate their programs and efforts in the light of the newly established purpose: **To bring people to maturity in Christ.**

Mary Collison, Emmanuel's director of discipleship, incorporated all the expertise and the training of others she could muster to maximize that critical and pivotal time for discipleship at all levels.

Benjamin Baker in his book *Shepherding the Sheep* continues:

> Administration is the task of discovering and clarifying the goals and purpose of the field it serves and moving in a coherent, comprehensive manner toward their realization. Such a definition suggests certain questions that any administrator must ask: What end or goal is to be served? What means will help reach the goal? How can all available resources and leadership be utilized in a coordinated and comprehensive movement toward the goal?[5]

Too often pastoral care as taught in seminaries and understood by laity and pastors alike is perceived as duties in the pastor's ministry. It is perceived by many pastors as an end in itself. If it is placed in the overall context of life and its pilgrimage, suddenly shepherding care in all forms takes on added dimension and new insight.

Thomas Herbert Conley has made this the central subject of his book *Pastoral Care for Personal Growth.*

> This book has, as an integral and foundational belief, the conviction that facilitating personal growth is not on the "fringes" of pastoral care but is the ultimate end. The final result of caring pastorally for persons and equipping them to be all that they can be in the Christian faith.[6]

5. *Ibid* p. 40.
6. Thomas Herbert Conley, *Pastoral Care for Personal Growth* (Valley Forge: Judson Press, 1977), p. 13.

Conley further states:

> But the most profound and pervasive need of the church
> today is to make disciples. Consistent, skilled, and dedi-
> cated pastoral care is one element of the total church min-
> istry that can help produce disciples.[7]

As the deacons of Emmanuel began to grasp the significance of the church's mission: "to bring people to maturity in Christ," it affected their prayers for Little Flock
members and it became the new grid through which they
read everything that related to the church.

Many became integrally involved in learning about discipleship from our director of discipleship. Lay shepherds
became involved in one-on-one discipleship ministries with
Little Flock members who expressed interest.

Christ's shepherding care effected the healing of a
wounded church. Shepherding ministries greatly contributed to this not only in extending pastoral care but in
discovering purpose and providing leadership in instructing and guiding the church membership toward achieving
that purpose.

It became a different church. Not only did Emmanuel
become a nurturing, caring habitat; it became a participatory body. Emmanuel was Christ's church, not a certain
pastor's church. In fact it *was* his church, and he was obviously forming it in a new pattern. It was beginning to
reflect his heart.

The former associate pastor and I had been meeting for
sharing, dialogue, and prayer on a consistent basis through
the years. The new fellowship was running aground and
some of the families returned to the Emmanuel Church.

In the fourth year of ministry, after discussing it with
me for several months, he requested a formal meeting with
the deacons of the Emmanuel Church. An evening meet-

7. *Ibid* p. 13.

ing was established. He brought with him a leading elder of the fellowship group, a former member, and a person who had been quite vocal in the days of the dissension.

The meeting in the lounge at Emmanuel between the seventeen deacons, the former associate, the leading elder of the fellowship group, and myself was an intense two-hour meeting. There was candor and clarification and further questions to clarify. There was honest reflection on feelings past and present expressed. Anger and feelings suppressed and buried were uncovered. It seemed like a marathon. Tears were shed. Finally forgiveness was sought from both sides. It was a powerful meeting obviously orchestrated under the control of the One who was shepherding his people and building and rebuilding his churches.

The conclusion of the evening was a beautiful close. In the middle of the room the two pastors of the two churches knelt. As we knelt side-by-side, I put my arm across the other pastor's back and he reciprocated. It was not artificial. Our times of prayer had linked us together long before that moment. The leading elder of the fellowship group laid hands on me and prayed for God's blessing on my ministry and that of the Emmanuel Church. Several deacons laid hands on the former associate pastor and prayed for him. Some were men who had expressed the deepest antipathy toward him. The rest of the deacons knelt around us and laid hands on the concentric circles of people nearer the center than they were. We were connected, united, and the Holy Spirit was joining us. It was one of those unique moments when the Great Shepherd by his Spirit laid hands on his undershepherds and made us one in him and for his service.

Healing happened. Emmanuel and those who dissented had come full circle. Forgiveness had been given. Now both groups were ready for his unrestricted blessing.

There was hugging and further forgiveness sought and given following the time of prayer when small groups of two and three and four formed.

Shepherding ministries with his style of compassionate care heals the brokenhearted and sets the captives free.

It was not an easy chapter in the experience of this shepherd, but it is one I wouldn't have missed. His shepherding care heals and makes wounded people and wounded churches whole.

11

Other Models of Shepherding Ministries

Dan Baumann in his book *All Originality Makes a Dull Church*, encourages pastors and churches to be gleaners: "Lessons learned by any local fellowship of believers ought to be common property of the entire body of Christ. Not to learn by the lessons of others is a waste of time and energy."[1]

This decade has produced a profuseness of group and shepherding ministries of considerable variety. Common trends of practices characterize most of them. People and environs and cultural patterns and personalities and varying leadership styles account for differing nuances in approach.

In this chapter there is a sampling of shepherding and group ministries that may catalyze some churches and pastors to an eclectic gleaning to form a shepherding approach to best minister to the needs of their respective flocks.

Elmbrook Church
Waukesha, Wisconsin
Senior Pastor: D. Stuart Briscoe

1. Dan Baumann, *All Originality Makes a Dull Church* (Santa Ana: Vision House, 1976), p. 21.

In a telephone interview Pastor Briscoe explained the experience of Elmbrook Church in the development of a small group ministry.

> *Beginning:* . . . We purchased a large map of the city, bought some pretty colored pins and stuck them in to represent the geographical location of each family. We divided the families into groups of approximately ten to fifteen and put a rubber band round the pins to represent "the group." We presented the map to the church, explaining our recommendation to establish small group ministries.
>
> *Response:* Reaction was mixed. One man said, "Don't try to tell me who my friends should be." To which I [Stuart Briscoe] replied, "I'm not. I'm trying to tell you who your brothers and sisters are." Another called the scheme "a Band-Aid," while some said, "It's the best thing to happen to the church in a long time."
>
> *The Time and Place:* Then came the big question, "When do you expect us to do all this?" asked one of the overworked minority.
>
> Taking a deep breath I answered, "How about Wednesday night?" In the ensuing horrified silence I added, "Only a fraction of the people come. They just sit and listen to me for most of the time and then listen to a few prayers for the rest of the time. And if the truth were known, it's all a bit of a bore."
>
> Eventually the Wednesday-night prayer meeting went the way of all deceased sacred cows. The people who wanted to pray met in their predestined groups and prayed.
>
> *Content:* For the first few weeks we made brief tapes for the groups and gave them questions for discussion. Later we weaned them from dependence on the pastors and encouraged them to get into other areas of interest with our supervision. It eventually became apparent to the people that they should do more than Bible study.
>
> Some asked for experiences that would encourage the believers to let down their guard a little so that they could begin to minister to one another's needs. This was exciting to some, threatening to others.
>
> *Benefits:* After three years, one group leader said, "We've

been together long enough that we don't pretend any-more. In fact, we dislike each other. But now we have two options. Either forget the whole thing and decide Christians can't get along or obey the Lord's command and love one another." They decided on the second op-tion and the group began to be what a church is intended to be. Nothing more or less than a unique society in the midst of fragmenting society.

Caution: Pastors who like to keep control of everything should not contemplate small-group ministries. Specta-tor-oriented churches should steer clear of this approach. Christians whose total spiritual ambition is to have "their needs met" should avoid this kind of experience."

Growth: I am convinced that those who are Christ's dis-ciples and desire to serve him will have ample opportu-nity in small groups to grow in every spiritual dimension along with those whom they are helping to grow.

Fellowship Bible Church
Dallas, Texas
Senior Pastor: Gene Getz

The Dispersed Church (in the homes). The minichurch concept is important at Fellowship Bible Church. When-ever twelve to fifteen new people come into the church they are formed into a minichurch led by a lay pastor-teacher, called an elder.

These minichurches meet a minimum of once a month for communion; most meet more often for prayer, Bible study, and sharing. Each week the elder calls his mini-church members (ten to twenty couples) to check on their spiritual progress and to learn of their prayer needs.

Being an elder at Fellowship Bible Church is more than meeting once a month to discuss church business. It in-volves weekly training from Getz and a commitment to ministry. Each elder as the pastor-teacher for his mini-church is to visit, encourage, counsel and teach the mem-bers of his group.[2]

2. Dan Baumann, *Ibid.* p. 53.

New Hope Community Church
Portland, Oregon
Senior Pastor: Dale E. Galloway

On October 14, 1972, Pastor Dale Galloway became the founding pastor of New Hope Community Church in Portland, Oregon. The growth since then has been phenomenal. Located on a spectacular 14 acres along I-205 freeway, the church ministers to more than 4,200 people each Sunday.

Key to the success of the church's ministry is a network of trained lay pastors and successful small groups. Following this procedure, the growing church has produced a one-on-one caring ministry.

Today, over 500 lay pastors lead more than 400 "Tender Loving Care" groups throughout the city each week.

The city is divided into four districts. Each district has a pastor and sectional pastor who supervises and equips lay pastors and their small groups for successful ministry and effective pastoral care.

The New Hope Community Church lists four ways their "Tender Loving Care" groups produce growth:

1. The heart-to-heart fellowship experienced in TLC groups is a different dynamic than in the Sunday celebration services. Participants are no longer members of an audience. They are known and know others by name—a feeling that they are an active part of the body of Christ.
2. Lay pastors are available for one-to-one care with counsel and prayer about specific needs. Besides being involved directly in evangelism and discipleship, our lay pastors are also keeping in contact with members who have become discouraged for a variety of reasons.
3. Spiritual gifts are exercised in building up the body of Christ and reaching the unsaved community. The TLC group recognizes that every believer is a priest unto the Lord.
4. Weekly Bible lessons are written by the senior pastor, Dale Galloway, taught by him to our lay pastors on Wednesday evening, and then used in their groups. This

systematic study of God's Word is not dependent on a few people who can write their own lesson plans. Because the pastor has central leadership in this ministry, tremendous unanimity flows through the life of the congregation.[3]

Stephen Ministries
1325 Roland
Saint Louis, Missouri 63117
Executive Director: Rev. Kenneth C. Haugk, Ph. D.

Emphasis: The Stephen Series is a system of training and organizing lay persons for caring ministry in and around their congregations.

History: In 1974 Dr. Kenneth Haugk, a minister who was also a clinical psychologist, was serving as associate pastor at Saint Stephen's Evangelical Lutheran church in Saint Louis, Missouri. Haugk was overwhelmed by the pastoral care workload.

The two streams of his life—community mental health and Christian theology—intermingled to suggest a solution to the problem of pastoral overload.

From mental-health work came a basic precept: professionals should not only provide direct treatment but serve as consultants to others. To Kenneth Haugk this sounded a lot like the relationship of pastor to people expressed in Ephesians: Pastors are "to prepare all God's people for the work of Christian service . . ." (Eph. 4:12 GOOD NEWS BIBLE).

He realized that we've had in the Christian church a lot of theological jargon about "the universal priesthood of all believers" and "equipping the saints for ministry" and "bearing one another's burdens" in the "body of Christ." He felt that, potentially, one of the most powerful support communities for helping people was their congregation. What would the church look like if people

3. Dale E. Galloway, *20-20 Vision—How to Create a Successful Church* (Portland: Scott Publishing Co., 1986)

really did minister to each other? What if it didn't depend so heavily on one overworked pastor? What if we could develop a whole church full of pastors?

Haugk gathered together a small group of people in his congregation and began to equip them to provide pastoral care (with a small *p*) to others. It was a modestly conceived program, to be limited to a ministry of lay caring within Saint Stephen's Church.

It worked so well that two of the lay care-givers urged that, "This is too good to keep to ourselves—we ought to think about sharing it with other congregations."

This is how Stephen ministry was formed. Now in its eighteenth year the record of the congregations in a broad spectrum of denominations trained in care giving by the Stephen ministries is impressive. Numerous seminars are held across the USA annually.

Two resource books *Christian Caregiving—A Way of Life*[4] and *Christian Caregiving—A Way of Life, Leaders' Guide* provide the textbooks for the Stephen ministries training.[5]

Calvary Baptist Church
1200 28th S.E.
Grand Rapids, Michigan 49508
(616) 243-3674
Senior Pastor: Dr. John White

Howard Bixby, former pastor of Calvary Baptist Church, was one of the pioneers in mobilizing the deacons of his church and training them in a ministry of caring. He and the church he led for years conducted Deacon Training Seminars. The present pastor, Dr. John White, has continued the program initiated by Dr. Howard Bixby.

Training cassettes and materials for individual and or group study may be secured from Church Development

4. Kenneth C. Haugk, *Christian Caregiving—A Way of Life* (Minneapolis: Augsburg, 1984)

5. Kenneth C. Haugk and William J. McKay. *Christian Caregiving—A Way of Life, Leaders' Guide* (Minneapolis: Augsburg, 1986)

Ministries, 147 Carol Drive, Clark Summit, PA 18411, Attn:
Dr. Howard Bixby.

A sample of the training cassettes are:

"The Biblical Blueprint for Deacons"
"Techniques and Methods for Being an Effective Deacon"
"A Deacon Looks at His Ministry"
"How a Deacon Ministers to Groups"
"How a Deacon Ministers to Individuals"
"How to Motivate and Lead in the Deacon Caring Ministry"

From the Deacon Couples Caring Ministry (Advanced
training including a wife's ministry) come the following
titles of cassettes:

"Ministering to the Bereaved or Suffering"
"Ministering to the Problem of Difficult People"
"Ways for Women to Use the Phone, Letters, and Personal
　Time to Minister"
"Ministering Through the Home"

New Heights Baptist Church
7913 N.E. 58th Avenue
Vancouver, Washington 98665
Senior Pastor: Dr. John A. Anderson

Home Bible Fellowships:

Leaders are carefully recruited and trained by the senior
pastor or the pastor of small groups. They, together with
their wives, actually form a group so that the training is
conducted in a typical situation in which they find themselves as leaders. Each trainee leads this group for two
weeks and is evaluated critically as part of the training.
Each training session includes a lesson on different aspects
of group leadership.

Once trained, a leader will either start his own group or
assume the leadership of an existing group. The groups
meet weekly in a home. No attempt is made to dictate
where anyone attends. The study time is not regarded as
a teaching situation, but as a Bible dialogue with the leader

occupying the role of facilitator. When groups reach fifteen to eighteen people in number, they are encouraged to divide and form another group.

The results of the program have been significant. There was significant numerical growth in the church and the Home Bible Fellowships significantly contributed to this. After their formation a spirit of love and ministry pervaded the church. The Bible-study method used is an inductive Bible study with emphasis on interpretation and appreciation.

The Home Bible Fellowship attenders testify to the positive impact the group experience had in their lives. Their testimonies include being cared for, being encouraged and growing in their knowledge of Scripture.

Touch Outreach Ministries
Box 19888
Houston, Texas 77224
(713)497-7901
President, Ralph W. Neighbor, Jr.

Since its beginning seventeen years ago, Ralph W. Neighbor, Jr., has served as President of Touch Outreach Ministries, an organization committed to equip pastors and lay leaders to use cell groups effectively in the local church.

Neighbor for years has been discovering, testing, and writing about small groups.

He has made extensive trips to observe cell groups in churches in Korea, South America, Australia, and in the USA. Neighbor has developed working models in Houston and Singapore and has consulted with scores of churches of many denominations.

Touch Outreach Ministries has pioneered in developing cell groups for use by those who serve the church as an organism rather than an organization.

According to Touch Outreach Ministries the church that lives as an organism will shape its lifestyle with these three Cs.

Celebration   The entire body of Christ meeting to worship their Lord and King.

Congregation   Composed of one hundred or less, these are
the subgroups of the body, gathering for Bible study and
growth.

Cells   Composed of no less than five and no more than
fifteen, these cells should exist in two forms: cells for
kinning and caring, and cells for witness and ministry

Neighbor promotes the establishment of two types of
cell groups. The first is for kinning (establishing family-
style relationships) and for caring. These groups invest their
time together creating bonds of love. It is here that persons
are affirmed, led to discover their ministry gifts and encouraged to serve one another.

He recommends that such groups should have a short
life span—from six to twelve months—before they multiply into two groups. Touch Outreach Ministries calls these
"Shepherd Group Cells."

The Shepherd Group Cell is composed of no more than
fifteen church members, meets monthly, and has an internal prayer chain.

Two outreach cell groups spawn from the kinning, caring cells. They are called: 1. *Visitation Cells*, which make
contact with those who visit the celebrations (services) or
the Congregations (adult Sunday-school classes). 2. *Share
Group Cells*, which make contact with those who will
never darken the doors of the church building.

The purpose of Touch Outreach Ministries is to equip
pastors and lay leaders to use cell groups effectively in the
local church.

Author's Observation

These are just samplings of many other creative shepherding and caring group ministries spawning around the
world in this decade.

Trends common to all identify them. These biblical

principles and their development is the theme of this book *A Caring Church: Through Shepherding Ministries.* The creative innovations of this chapter should encourage each pastor and church leader to creatively adapt ideas and materials to his local church situation rather than simply reproduce any one of them as a "canned program."

12

Shepherding:
A Scriptural Perspective

The Christian faith, which I embrace, originates in revelation. Revelation comes to man in two forms: natural and supernatural. Because all people are spiritually blind, natural revelation fails to give a reliable knowledge of spiritual things.

To offset this lack of knowledge, God discloses himself in supernatural revelation. This is set forth clearly in the Bible. This God-breathed revelation is infallible. It is wholly trustworthy in matters of history and doctrine.

Nor do we need to do more than remind ourselves that this attitude of entire trust in every word of the scriptures has been characteristic of the people of God from the very foundation of the church. Christendom has always reposed upon the belief that the utterances of this book are properly oracles of God.[1]

The man who shepherds in the manner God intended comes to God's Word for truth and instruction. In the Old Testament Yahweh is pictured as the Shepherd of Israel. In

1. Benjamin B. Warfield, *The Inspiration and Authority of the Bible* (Philadelphia: The Presbyterian and Reformed Publishing Co., 1948), p. 107.

the New Testament Jesus describes himself as the Good
Shepherd. He trained his apostles to be shepherds of people. Apostles then taught and trained congregational leaders, overseers, elders, and deacons, in the leadership,
feeding, and care of the people of the New Testament
church.

Yahweh as the Shepherd of Israel

The Old Testament pictures Yahweh as the Shepherd of
Israel. The first Old Testament reference to Yahweh as a
shepherd is Jacob's blessing for the sons of Joseph:

> May the God before whom my fathers Abraham and Isaac
> walked, the God who has been my Shepherd all my life to
> this day, the Angel who has delivered me from all harm—
> may he bless these boys (Gen. 48:15, 16).

The Old Testament is replete with this image of Yahweh.

> In the Old Testament the description of Yahweh as the
> Shepherd of Israel is ancient usage, but the surprising pau-
> city of references in which the title is used of Yahweh shows
> that this is not just a formal divine prediction. The appli-
> cation of the shepherd image to Yahweh is embedded in
> the living piety of Israel.[2]

The psalmist David had been a shepherd and became
known as the "Shepherd King" of Israel. He authored the
Twenty-third Psalm which begins, "The LORD is my shepherd." The Lord who dominates the psalm is Yahweh, the
Lord God of Israel.

2. Kittel and Friedrich, *Theological Dictionary of the New Testament*,
4:487.

Yahweh, as the God who led Israel out of Egypt, is addressed in the metaphor of shepherd in Psalm 80:1, 2.

Hear us, O Shepherd of Israel,
you who lead Joseph like a flock; you who sit enthroned
   between the cherubim, shine forth
before Ephraim, Benjamin and Manasseh.
Awaken your might;
come and save us.

The prophets write of the covenantal relationship in pastoral terms.

For this is what the Sovereign LORD says: I myself will search for my sheep and look after them. As a shepherd looks after his scattered flock when he is with them, so will I look after my sheep. I will rescue them from all the places where they were scattered on a day of clouds and darkness (Ezek. 34:11).

Yahweh was pictured in the metaphor of a human shepherd. However, the Hebrew rightfully thought of God as Spirit. The concept of Yahweh the shepherd was sometimes difficult to understand. Because Yahweh's representative shepherds failed to be good shepherds, they tarnished the image.

The Sovereign Lord spoke of such shepherds through Ezekiel, "Woe to the shepherds of Israel who only take care of themselves! Should not shepherds take care of the flock?" (Ezek. 34:2).

Charles Jefferson aptly describes the period prior to the Good Shepherd's coming.

But while there was a good shepherd in the skies, there was no good shepherd on the earth. All the shepherds of Israel, one after another, proved disappointing. They did not do their duty. They failed to feed the flock. They did not wisely

guide it. They could not save it. But the Hebrew heart did
not despair. It dared to dream of an ideal shepherd who
would surely come. A Messiah had been promised, and he
would be a shepherd. He would guide and feed and save the
sheep.[3]

Yahweh caring for his sheep comes into focus in the
progressive revelation of Scripture. In the New Testament
Jesus presents himself as the Good Shepherd.

Jesus as the Good Shepherd

The Son of God in human form came describing himself
as the Good Shepherd (John 10:11–18):

The name "pastoral" is a uniquely Christian term that expresses a fundamental concept that is deeply imbedded in
every Biblical portrayal of Christian ministry. The term
refers to a rich scripture figure that finds its beginning and
end in God. He, who is the "Shepherd of Israel" (Psalm
80:1), ultimately demonstrated the meaning of His covenantal love as The Great Shepherd of the sheep by giving
His life for them.[4]

The term *shepherd* seemed to come into its own when
Jesus appeared. He took the title on himself. Jesus never
called himself a priest, a preacher, a bishop, or an elder,
but apparently liked to think of himself as a shepherd.

He presented himself as a good shepherd, one who really
cared for his sheep, in contrast to "hired hands" who cared
nothing. When the wolf came, the hired hand abandoned
the sheep and ran away. Jesus declared, "I am the good

3. Jefferson, *The Minister as Shepherd*, p. 15.
4. Adams, *The Pastoral Life*, p. 5.

shepherd; I know my sheep and my sheep know me . . .
and I lay down my life for the sheep" (John 10:14, 15).

The ministry of Jesus embodied relationship to others
by shepherding. Wherever he went, people needed his kind
of care:

> In the sixth chapter of Mark's gospel we find Him taking
> a day off with His disciples. Nobody needed it more than
> He. But when they reached their destination, a quiet desert
> retreat, they found it no longer private, but overrun with
> people. People who wouldn't let well enough alone. People
> so rude and inconsiderate that they didn't even apologize
> for aborting His plans for much needed rest and relaxation.
> Certainly He would have been justified in telling them to
> "get lost!" After all, enough is enough. But He didn't. He
> couldn't. "And Jesus, when he came out, saw much people,
> and was moved with compassion toward them, because
> they were as sheep not having a shepherd: and he began to
> teach them many things" (Mark 6:34 KJV).[5]

Jesus, as the Shepherd-Savior, has an unusual appeal.
Thousands who have lived a lifetime removed from contact with sheep are drawn into the metaphor. Jesus told of
the shepherd searching for the one lost sheep. People identify with that lost sheep.

There is a personal appeal in a hymn that is sung around
the world.

> Savior, like a shepherd lead us,
>   Much we need thy tender care;
> In thy pleasant pastures feed us;
>   For our use thy folds prepare.[6]

5. Eugene L. Stowe, *The Ministry of Shepherding* (Kansas City: Beacon Hill
Press, 1976), p. 19.

6. Dorothy A. Thrupp, "Savior, Like a Shepherd Lead Us," *Worship and
Service Hymnal* (Chicago: Hope Publishing Co., 1960), p. 500.

Apostles as Shepherds

Jesus was aware of the need to prepare shepherds and workers.

When he saw the crowds, he had compassion on them, because they were harassed and helpless, like sheep without a shepherd. Then he said to his disciples, "The harvest is plentiful but the workers are few. Ask the Lord of the harvest, therefore, to send out workers into his harvest field" (Matt. 9:36–38).

During his earthly ministry Jesus commissioned twelve disciples for a special role. Mark says, "He appointed twelve—designating them apostles—that they might be with him and that he might send them out to preach and to have authority to drive out demons" (Mark 3:14, 15).

The Twelve performed three functions, while they were with Jesus. They were with him as companions until his death. The second function was preaching. Mark 6:12 uses the term *keryssein,* which is translated, "to preach" or "to proclaim." But Mark 6:30 says, "The apostles gathered around Jesus and reported to him all they had done and taught [*edidaxan*]."

The postresurrection teaching ministry, including the apostles' doctrine (Acts 2:42), can be traced back to this beginning. The third function was to exercise authority over evil spirits (Mark 6:7). Mark 6:13 adds to that authority over evil spirits, anointing and healing of sick people.

Each function of preaching and teaching, and delivery from satanic oppression with healing, is rudimental to shepherding people in the name of Christ.

Jefferson refers to the poignant scene by the seaside where Jesus restored his apostle, Simon Peter.

The history of the church began with Jesus saying to the leader who is to head the work of discipling the nations: "I am a shepherd, be thou a shepherd, too."

Testing Simon Peter's love, Jesus said:

> "Feed my lambs . . .
> Take care of my sheep . . .
> Feed my sheep . . ." (John 21:15–17).[7]

Following Christ's death, resurrection, and ascension, the leading persons among Christ's followers were the apostles. There were eleven following the betrayal and demise of Judas Iscariot. Matthias was chosen to complete the Twelve. During replacement Peter, in Acts 1:20, said in reference to Judas Iscariot, "May another take his place of leadership [*episkope*]."

If there were no other evidence, this statement substantiates the apostles as shepherds.

> To carry on the work of an overseer (*episkopos,* "bishop") does not mean to do the work of any sort of overseer in general, but in the New Testament it always carries the idea of overseeing *as a shepherd.* It involves the all-embracing oversight required by the descriptions of such in Psalm 23, John 10 and elsewhere.[8]

The importance of the twelve apostles in the formative stages of the church in Jerusalem can hardly be overstated. In the truest sense they were the shepherds of the small growing movement.

Undoubtedly the first apostolic men of the primitive community also governed that community, possessed special

---

7. Jefferson, *The Minister as Shepherd,* p. 10.
8. Adams, *The Pastoral Life,* p. 8.

honor within it, and took decision concerning it. The vital meaning of Christian witness, embracing as it does the whole of life, would certainly lead us to assume this, and Paul and Luke confirm it.[9]

As mentioned earlier, a crucial part of shepherding in the formative church's existence was the teaching, feeding ministry by the apostles.

> Those who accepted his message were baptized, and about three thousand were added to their number that day. They devoted themselves to the apostles' teaching and to the fellowship, to the breaking of bread and to prayer (Acts 2:41–42).

> So the Twelve gathered all the disciples together and said, "It would not be right for us to neglect the ministry of the word of God in order to wait on tables. Brothers, choose seven men from among you who are known to be full of the Spirit and wisdom. We will turn this responsibility over to them and will give our attention to prayer and the ministry of the word" (Acts 6:2–4).

At the church in Jerusalem, Peter emerged as the natural leader of the community. Peter with the apostles ruled and governed the affairs of the primitive Christian community. The Twelve taught the "teaching of the apostles"; they received gifts to be distributed in the community of believers, and they provided leadership. Outside Jerusalem they assisted by sending Peter and John to Samaria to a newly forming church.

In the term *apostle* (New Testament usage) there is a distinction between the Twelve and general use of the term.

> In fact, for Paul "apostles" are not only the twelve: Andronicus and Junias are "outstanding among the apostles"

---

9. Hans von Campenhausen, *Ecclesiastical Authority and Spiritual Power* (Stanford: Stanford University Press, 1969), p. 27.

(Rom. 16:7), where "the apostles" already appear as a category of office of the community (1 Cor. 12:28f; Eph. 2:20; 4:11). . . . In other words, around A.D. 55 there already were many "apostles" who were not of the twelve. This notion of apostle (one not of the twelve) certainly applies to Paul himself and, very likely to many other unspecified "apostles."[10]

Paul emerges as a particular apostle. While most persons apart from the Twelve are referred to as apostles in the functional sense alone, this is not true of Paul. Though he was not one of the Twelve, Scripture indicates he had a unique calling. He was the apostle to proclaim the gospel to the Gentiles, Christ's particular representative to the non-Jew.

But when God, who set me apart from birth and called me by his grace, was pleased to reveal his Son in me so that I might preach him among the Gentiles, I did not consult any man, nor did I go up to Jerusalem to see those who were apostles before I was, but I went immediately into Arabia and later returned to Damascus (Gal. 1:15–17).

Paul became an overseeing shepherd to all the churches he established in Gentile territory:

Paul knows that his congregations need him, and cannot as yet do without him, and his disquiet increases when alien, destructive influences seek to intrude between him and his people. Moreover, the nature of his relationship with them seems to be such that there is no reason why it need come to an end. . . . The relationship is thus a permanent and reciprocal one, which will reach its term only at the last day.[11]

10. Miguens, *Church Ministries in New Testament Times*, p. 25.
11. von Campenhausen, *Ecclesiastical Authority and Spiritual Power*, pp. 44, 45.

The tender care of the apostles in the first-century church is graphically depicted by the apostle Paul.

> As apostles of Christ we could have been a burden to you, but we were gentle among you, like a mother caring for her little children. We loved you so much that we were delighted to share with you not only the gospel of God but our lives as well, because you had become so dear to us (1 Thess. 2:7, 8).

Overseers and Elders as Shepherds

The Greek word *episkopos* means "overseer" or "bishop." In 1 Peter 2:25 Christ himself is called *episkopos*. The conception of Good Shepherd and overseer of his church are closely related.

> In general, the terms ποιμαινεω and ἐπισκοπειν were closely linked in describing the work of the shepherd.... The phrase "Shepherd and bishop of your souls" carries within it all that is said by Greek speaking Gentiles and Jews about God as ἐπίσκοπος. As suggested by the context, which points us to the deepest mysteries of salvation history, ἐπίσκοπος is thus a title of majesty ascribed to Jesus in his work in relation to the community.[12]

The term *episkopos* was applied to the leaders in the first-century church. They were overseeing or supervising in Christ's place. Usage in early history described function as a supervising leader rather than a fixed office. Paul addressed the elders of the Ephesian church telling them that God had made them overseers.

> Guard yourselves and all the flock of which the Holy Spirit has made you overseers. Be shepherds of the church of God, which he bought with his own blood (Acts 20:28).

12. Kittel and Friedrich, *Theological Dictionary of the New Testament*, 2:615.

The first Christian use of *episkopos* was in the Helle-nistic churches located in Gentile territory. A secular use of the term had origins in Greek culture. Quite naturally the word was adapted to the overseers and supervisors of Christian churches in that setting. Prior to Paul's pastoral letters several leaders in each congregation were recog-nized and addressed as bishops and overseers.

Initially, several bishops or overseers shared the respon-sibility of leadership in each church. There is the sugges-tion in Paul's pastoral letter to Timothy, in 1 Timothy 3:2, that the overseer was a single position in that local church. Responsibilities of overseers were similar to those of pas-tors in the twentieth century.

The Greek word *presbyteros* means elder. The original meaning had reference to men with maturity and spiritual experience. The Jews traced the beginning of eldership back to the time of Moses. When the burden of leadership became too heavy to bear, seventy "elders" were gifted with the Spirit which had rested exclusively on Moses. After that time eldership was incorporated into Jewish tra-dition becoming a permanent fixture in the Hebrew reli-gious community. The primitive Christian churches organized themselves along Judaistic lines that they had always known.

> The system of elders is therefore probably of Judaeo-Chris-tian origin, just as bishops and deacons were at first at home only in Gentile Christian congregations.[13]

Though the term *presbyteros* was carried over from the Jewish community, the role of Christian elders was quite different from the very beginning.

There were similarities. Elders of the Christian com-munity had charge of the financial administration of each church. It was to the local elders that Paul and Barnabas delivered money sent to relieve the poor brothers of Jeru-salem during the famine.

13. Von Campenhausen, *Ecclesiastical Authority and Spiritual Power*, p. 77.

Jewish elders had exercised order and discipline over members of their synagogue. Christian elders comprised the council of the Judaeo-Christian church.

> They, together with the apostles, are the representatives of the local community of Jerusalem to receive envoys from other communities (Acts 15:4); they, together with the apostles, form the supreme court of appeals on questions concerning doctrine and, as a result, practical life among Christians (Acts 15:2, 6, 22, 23; 16:4); in Acts 21:18 they appear as the senate of only one leader, James.[14]

There are marked dissimilarities too. Personal compassion and care were unknown among the Jewish elders. This is the pastoral aspect alluded to by James, prominent elder in the Jerusalem Christian community. In James 5:13–16, James gave shepherding instruction for his elders. In sickness the elders were to anoint with oil "in the name of the LORD" for restoration. James implies that elders were to act as confessors and intercessors. They had a responsibility not only for those ailing physically, but also for the spiritually weak.

The elders, ministering "in the name of the LORD," were continuing the shepherding ministry of Jesus. He was using their hands to touch the helpless and the harassed.

There was another marked difference between elders of the Jewish synagogues and those of Christian assemblies. Elders of the synagogue were administrators, not preachers or teachers.

> The elders were the administrators of the synagogue; they did not preach, but they saw to the good government and order of the synagogue and then exercised discipline over its members.[15]

---

14. Miguens, *Church Ministries in New Testament Times*, p. 39.
15. William Barclay, *The Letters of James and Peter* (Philadelphia: Westminster Press, 1977), p. 263.

The elders of the church were responsible for sound doctrine. This was apparent, as dangers to the new movement increased.

In the twentieth chapter of Acts, Paul arranged for the elders of Ephesus to meet him in Miletus. The apostle's primary concern was a developing crisis with reference to the doctrine of unadulterated truth. Paul charged the elders to watch lest the flock be led astray and destroyed.

> Guard yourselves and all the flock of which the Holy Spirit has made you overseers. Be shepherds of the church of God, which he bought with his own blood. I know that after I leave, savage wolves will come in among you and will not spare the flock. Even from your own number men will arise and distort the truth in order to draw away disciples after them. So be on your guard! (Acts 20:28–31).

Function of overseers in Hellenistic territories and elders in the Judaeo community was the same. The terms applied were the difference. Prior to the council in Jerusalem, designations and distinctions of Hellenistic or Jewish extraction are fairly easy to differentiate. Then the congregations mingled and interpenetrated so that the terms *elder-presbyteros*, and *overseer-episkopos*, were used synonymously and interchangeably.

In their study of organizational life, pastoral epistles offered the last word of the New Testament period. The ambiguity of the term *elder* and *overseer* continued.

In the first letter to Timothy, offices of overseer and deacon appear to be highly developed. The apostle went into detail about necessary qualifications for the offices of overseer and deacon. Two qualities are noteworthy in the 1 Timothy 3 passage. The overseer is presented in the singular (elsewhere elders and overseers have been regarded as several in number). The second matter is that the term *elder* is conspicuous by its absence. It seems that it has been assimilated and incorporated into the office of overseer.

Another pastoral epistle penned by Paul from the same period of his ministry is addressed to Titus. Paul instructs Titus to appoint elders in every town. In that letter, Titus 1:7, the apostle identifies the work of an appointed elder as an overseer entrusted with God's work. In that same passage Paul elaborates on the feeding shepherd dispensing God's truth.

> He must hold firmly to the trustworthy message as it has been taught, so that he can encourage others by sound doctrine and refute those who oppose it (Titus 1:9).

Whatever the designation, elder or overseer, these leaders were to display the same leadership among the flock that Jesus would. By his Spirit he empowered elders and overseers who ministered with his shepherd heart "in his name."

Deacons as Shepherds

The English word *deacon* comes from the Greek noun *diakonos* which occurs twenty-eight times in the New Testament. The related feminine noun *diakonia* occurs thirty-two times. The noun form means waiter, servant, helper, and minister. The verb *diakoneo* meaning to wait on tables, serve, and minister, is used thirty-nine times in the New Testament.

Many of these New Testament references are not in relationship to the role of a deacon in a church. Most were directed to servants' work, waiting on tables, helping or serving other persons. This is what the word *diakonos* meant. Society viewed it as a lowly demeaning job, humiliating to the person performing the service.

Jesus took those humiliating connotations and lifted them, declaring that it was the highest way to live. He spoke of himself in this language. Mark 10:45 might be translated, "For even the son of man did not come to be deaconed, but to deacon, and to give his life as a ransom for many."

It was to this style of living that Jesus called his disciples. The essence of the disciple life was to serve and minister to others.

Each believer, indwelt by the Spirit of Christ, has the heart of a shepherd. Having the heart of a servant-deacon is the essence of Jesus, so every believer is directed in Christ's stead.

The church selects members to be its Board of Deacons. This never cancels the responsibility of every Christian to live the servant life.

The seven men of Acts 6:1–6 were chosen like the twentieth-century deacon to provide leadership, care, and concern. The "harassed and helpless, like sheep without a shepherd" of Jesus' day, were in the same category as people today.

Those of Acts 6 have been viewed as the first group of deacons, even if unnamed in Scripture. Some scholars have made an issue of the absence of the term. Regardless of the absence, the function of deacon is evident.

It should be emphasized, however, that in all later centuries this passage in Acts 6 has done more to shape the idea men form about deacons than any other Biblical passage.[16]

In Philippians 1:1, Paul mentioned two groups of leaders in the church in Philippi. One is comprised of bishops or overseers. They were the officers governing and leading the local church. The other group contained deacons who were the helpful servants and ministers. These, too, were officers and leaders of the local church.

In 1 Timothy 3:1–13, Paul refers to the same two kinds of officials in the local church. In this passage the office

16. Floyd V. Filson, "Lay Ordination" (Faith & Order Commission, World Council of Churches, July, 1963), p. 6. (Mimeographed.)

of bishop is singular. Scholars suggest that one overseer was already established practice, becoming fully developed in the patristic period. It appears that the overseer Paul describes has qualifications similar to pastor of a local contemporary church.

In contrast, the group of deacons was plural. The passage references a list of personal qualities for deacon but gives no description of the duties.

> Amazingly little is said as to their duties. It is from Acts 6, not from Philippians 1:1 or 1 Timothy 3:8–13 that the church has taken the conception of the deacon as combining duties in relief work, preaching, and administering the sacraments.[17]

As the church moved into the patristic period, through the first two decades of the second century, the function of the church offices crystallized. A fixed order became more pronounced. Because there were no church buildings, groups of Christians met in homes and other available places. The bishop became leader of all small congregations throughout each city.

The Pauline letters addressed to specific churches were read by numerous small congregations of the church in that city. These small groups needed to express their unity. This was accomplished through the overseeing bishop.

The three offices, bishop, elders, and deacons, were clearly delineated in the patristic writings of the second century. Ignatius of Antioch wrote that these three offices were a necessary essential structure in the church.

> You should honor all the deacons like Jesus Christ, the bishop like the image of the Father, and the elders as the council of God and the gathering of the apostles. Without these one cannot talk of the church (Trall. 3:1).[18]

17. Ibid., p. 7.
18. Lukas Vischer, "The Problem of the Diaconate" (Faith & Order Commission, World Council of Churches, July, 1963), p. 5. (Mimeographed.)

Elders and deacons of each congregation became leaders under authority of their local overseer or bishop. The elders became leaders, administrators, and teachers of the small congregations. There was merely a short step between this and the developing priesthood.

This brought the deacons into touch with the bishop. His concern for the unity of the church and for the meeting of human need led to close ties between the bishop and the deacons. If, as seems to have been the case, the common meals of the church were a means of giving relief to needy Christians, and the deacons had duties in connection with those common meals, and if those common meals recalled Jesus' meals with his disciples and especially his Last Supper with them, it can be seen that this would further close ties of the deacon with the bishop, who would be in charge of the sacraments.[19]

The next historic development for the deacon was to view his office as the first advancement to the priesthood. Two things had happened. The deacon was no longer a lay person, in our present use of that term. Of greater gravity was the movement away from the care-giving function of the office. The deacon's duties came to be preparing for the priesthood lying ahead for him. The attending-to-needs function lost its importance as a vital role while the deacon worked on eligibility to become a priest. Liturgical and administrative functions became preeminent.

Unfortunately this care-giving work of today's deacon is still minimal in function. The role has been reduced to Thanksgiving baskets, and special relief when the Department of Welfare is slow or unable to act.

There is a trend in baptistic and evangelical churches to fortify the Board of Elders. This minimizes the Board of Deacons or reduces it to trustee status. History indicates that churches and movements following this pattern al-

---

19. Floyd V. Filson, "Lay Ordination" (Chicago: 1964), p. 10. (Mimeographed.)

most inevitably have a strong Board of Elders. They govern and administer the business affairs of the church while the overseeing of souls is neglected.

The term *servant-diakonos,* assures an attitude which will "not lord it over those entrusted to you" (1 Peter 5:3):

> It is interesting to notice that this word "deacon," which from the first has implied some form of leadership, does not carry the connotation of power and prominence. This simple, ordinary word for service is used to speak of Christ's service to men and of the service owed one who is a Christian to God, to Christ, and to his fellows. In this way the New Testament clarifies the pastoral character which should be the mark of the church, corporately as a total people of God, and individually, both in places of leadership and in the private responsibility one bears in life. This concept of service makes all Christian leaders servants of servants, supporting them, leading, counselling, and instructing them in their ministries.[20]

There is much of the shepherd's caring compassion in a deacon's ministry. If his care-giving ministry could be continued with spiritual guidance, then the quality of shepherding helpless harassed people would become the shepherding Jesus intended.

The term *servant-diakonos* has potential in today's contemporary church.

> The Greek language offered many designations from personal or cultic associations for the Church's office, but instead of accepting these the Church developed a new designation which was common to neither the Jewish nor the Hellenistic environment, διαχονία "service" or διαχονεῖν "to serve." Since this term occurs in the Synoptic as well as the Pauline terminology, it was already present in all the Early Apostolic Church. It was the usual term for

20. Donald F. Thomas, *The Deacon in a Changing Church* (Valley Forge: Judson Press, 1969), p. 19.

functions within the framework of the Church and not, significantly enough, for the services of one's neighbor or within the social orders. Διαχονία is the service performed for the unifying and preservation of the Church, the service which establishes and maintains the faith; thus it is the office of the Church.[21]

God is speaking to today's church. The revelation is *his* speaking voice.

This "good shepherd in the skies" yearns to shepherd people to himself. He desires to guide, feed, and save people who are his sheep.

In the Old Testament, the Father is pictured as the Shepherd of Israel. In the New Testament, Jesus described himself as the Good Shepherd. He trained his apostles to be shepherds of people. The apostles taught church leaders, overseers, elders and deacons in the shepherding ministry.

It is through the same leaders, today, that Christ continues his shepherding ministry.

21. Leonard Goppelt, *Apostolic and Post-Apostolic Times*, Trans. Robert A. Guelich (London: Adam & Charles Black, 1970), p. 177.

Appendixes

Appendix 1

An Affirmation of Our Faith

Adopted by the Baptist General Conference in 1951

1. THE WORD OF GOD

We believe that the Bible is the Word of God, fully inspired and without error in the original manuscripts, written under the inspiration of the Holy Spirit, and that it has supreme authority in all matters of faith and conduct.

2. THE TRINITY

We believe that there is one living and true God, eternally existing in three persons; that these are equal in every divine perfection, and that they execute distinct but harmonious offices in the work of creation, providence and redemption.

3. GOD THE FATHER

We believe in God, the Father, an infinite, personal spirit, perfect in holiness, wisdom, power and love. We believe that He concerns Himself mercifully in the affairs of men, that He hears and answers prayer, and that He saves from sin and death all who come to him through Jesus Christ.

4. JESUS CHRIST

We believe in Jesus Christ, God's only begotten Son, conceived by the Holy Spirit. We believe in His virgin birth, sinless life, miracles and teachings. We believe in His substitutionary atoning death, bodily resurrection, ascension into heaven, perpetual intercession for His people, and personal visible return to earth.

5. THE HOLY SPIRIT

We believe in the Holy Spirit who came forth from the Father and Son to convict the world of sin, righteousness, and judgment, and to regenerate, sanctify, and empower all who believe in Jesus Christ. We believe that the Holy Spirit indwells every believer in Christ, and that He is an abiding helper, teacher and guide.

6. REGENERATION

We believe that all men are sinners by nature and by choice and are, therefore, under condemnation. We believe that those who repent of their sins and trust in Jesus Christ as Savior are regenerated by the Holy Spirit.

7. THE CHURCH

We believe in the universal church, a living spiritual body of which Christ is the head and all regenerated persons are members. We believe in the local church, consisting of a company of believers in Jesus Christ, baptized on a credible profession of faith, and associated for worship, work and fellowship. We believe that God has laid upon the members of the local church the primary task of giving the Gospel of Jesus Christ to a lost world.

8. CHRISTIAN CONDUCT

We believe that a Christian should live for the glory of God and the well-being of his fellowmen; that his conduct should be blameless before the world; that he should be a faithful steward of his possessions; and that he should seek to realize for himself and others the full stature of maturity in Christ.

9. The Ordinances

We believe that the Lord Jesus Christ has committed two ordinances to the local church, baptism and the Lord's Supper. We believe that Christian baptism is the immersion of a believer in water into the name of the triune God. We believe that the Lord's Supper was instituted by Christ for commemoration of His death. We believe that these two ordinances should be observed and administered until the return of the Lord Jesus Christ.

10. Religious Liberty

We believe that every human being has direct relations with God, and is responsible to God alone in all matters of faith; that each church is independent and must be free from interference by any ecclesiastical or political authority; that therefore Church and State must be kept separate as having different functions, each fulfilling its duties free from dictation or patronage of the other.

11. Church Cooperation

We believe that local churches can best promote the cause of Jesus Christ by cooperating with one another in a denominational organization. Such an organization, whether a regional or district conference, exists and functions by the will of the churches. Cooperation in a conference is voluntary and may be terminated at any time. Churches may likewise cooperate with interdenominational fellowships on a voluntary independent basis.

12. The Last Things

We believe in the personal and visible return of the Lord Jesus Christ to earth and the establishment of His kingdom. We believe in the resurrection of the body, the final judgment, the eternal felicity of the righteous, and the endless suffering of the wicked.

Appendix 2

Bible Reading

Paragraph Title Record

THURSDAY. Date_____ Today's paragraph_____
1. Main idea of the paragraph in title form (eight words or less)

TITLE:_____

_____

2. The idea's application to my life:_____

_____

_____

FRIDAY.   Date_____ Today's paragraph_____
1. Main idea of the paragraph in title form (eight words or less)

TITLE:_____

_____

2. The idea's application to my life:_____

_____

_____

SATURDAY. Date_____ Today's paragraph_____
1. Main idea of the paragraph in title form (eight words or less)

TITLE:_____

_____

2. The idea's application to my life:_____

_____

_____

Appendix 3

Little Flock Section

Basic Requirements for *Overseeing* Your Little Flock

1. A minimum of a corporate little flock gathering at least once each three months.
   a. This will be primarily social with its objective the building of relationships to develop a support group for the members of the little flock.
   b. It can be a covered dish dinner. A church facility can be used. Backyard home gatherings are better as the weather permits. Picnic, ball games, and other group interest opportunities can be used.
2. The establishment of a meaningful pastoral relationship between the lay shepherd and each member of his flock. The members of the flock, in time, will turn to the lay shepherds first in crisis. Then the lay shepherds will contact the church office and pastoral staff.
3. A hospital call must be made by the lay shepherd on each member of his little flock who is hospitalized. Books to take as gifts will be available. They are in the closet behind the bifold doors in the conference room (or wherever is feasible).
4. One man and his wife are to be selected by the shepherding team to be discipled as understudies in shepherding. This will require at least a monthly meeting with the understudies to share in brief the general content of the weekly training sessions and share and pray for the needs of the little flock as well as plan a future ministry to them.
5. A home-communion service with the little flock led by the lay shepherd will be held at least once each year.

Appendix 4

Report Form of Little Flock Ministries by the Shepherding Teams

1. This form may be filled out by the deacon or deaconess. Please collaborate on the material put down.
2. Next Wednesday evening, April 25, will be report night. All deacons and deaconesses are urged to be in attendance. Either the deacon or deaconess will share in summary the material of the year's activities from the report form. Dessert will be served—it should be a good evening. If you cannot be there, see that the report is in the office by May 1.
3. List the approximate dates of times you've had Little Flock get-togethers, what they were (potlucks, and so forth) and the approximate number in attendance.

   _____ _____ _____

   _____ _____ _____

   _____ _____ _____

4. List individual ministries that you can recall like home calls, hospital calls, luncheon appointments, telephone calls, and so forth.

   _____

   _____

   _____

   _____

   _____

   _____

5. Write a paragraph about one shepherding incident in your Little Flock ministry that was especially rewarding and heartwarming to you.

Appendix 5

Shepherding Report

Visit Little Flock Home

Date_____

Shepherding team_____

Home visited_____

Evaluate call_____

_____

_____

_____

_____

_____

_____

_____

_____

_____

Scripture used_____

Check if closed with prayer _____

Reflection—what spiritual needs surfaced or were made more apparent to you because of the call: _____

_____

_____

Signed:

_____

Appendix 6

Understanding the Role of the Undershepherding Team

EXODUS 18:24; 2 TIMOTHY 2:2

The shepherding team will select another husband-wife combination to work as helpers in various ministries to the flock.

1. This ministry may lead to a full shepherding role with election as a deacon and deaconess, but it isn't necessarily a first step in that direction. The assisting team may be chosen because of their gifts which would augment those of the shepherding team. For example, the shepherdess does not feel strong gifts in entertaining or organizing for dinners and social affairs. A man doesn't feel strong alone. They see a couple that have both these gifts and would be willing to serve in those areas and assist. They are asked to do so.

2. It would be a tremendous help to the shepherding team if they would share the responsibility of the flock with the undershepherding team. With the shepherding teams taking six households and the undershepherding teams six households for fellowship or prayer gatherings, the division of labor and a more flexible grouping would be the result.

3. Perhaps the shepherding team and the undershepherding team could share the list, six and six for telephoning. Checking up in case of absence, illness, and so forth.

4. A once-a-month meeting with the two teams would enable the shepherd and shepherdess to share the Wednesday-night training session and what is taking place there. It would also enable them to begin discipling the undershepherding team if they are responsive.

Appendix 7

Network of Lay-Shepherding Ministry

Appendix 8

Sunday School Class
1. Taught by teacher
2. Organized for visitation
3. Organized for social fellowship
4. Attended by deacons/deaconess as shepherds and as a liaison to little flocks

Little Flocks
1. Overseen by lay shepherds
2. Organized for pastoral care and as a support group
3. Organized for prayer
4. Organized for home communion and worship service
5. Combined with other little flocks for a growth group

Growth Group
1. Supervised by corps of lay shepherds
2. Led by a leader or leaders
3. Meet every other week or monthly in homes for Bible study, sharing and prayer.

Bibliography

Books

Adams, Jay E. *Pastoral Leadership.* Grand Rapids: Baker Book House, 1975.
The third in a series under the overarching theme, "Shepherding God's Flock." The book is addressed to pastors, but the principles of the book and much of its material is applicable to lay leaders.

Adams, Jay E. *The Pastoral Life.* Grand Rapids: Baker Book House, 1975.
This is the first in a series on shepherding God's flock. It introduces the subject of pastoral theology and then gives a very good overview of shepherd life and care. It is addressed to pastors.

Baker, Benjamin S., *Shepherding the Sheep.* Nashville: Broadman, 1983.
The author, a successful pastor of a black church writes to black pastors. Some material is targeted to pastors with limited training, but in general provides an excellent resource for training in pastoral care and skills.

Barclay, William. *The Letters of James and Peter.* Philadelphia: Westminster Press, 1977.

Baumann, Dan. *All Originality Makes a Dull Church.* Santa Ana, Calif.: Vision House Publishers, 1976.
The author depicts five styles of churches, giving a case study on nine. He believes that all lessons learned by a local fellowship ought to be common property of the body of Christ.

Clebsch, William A., and Jaekle, Charles R. *Pastoral Care in Historical Perspective.* Englewood Cliffs, N.J.: Prentice Hall, 1964.
The book has excellent definitions of pastoral care from a technical perspective.

Detwiler-Zapp, Diane and William Caveness Dixon, *Lay Caregiving.* Philadelphia: Fortress Press, 1982.
A professional psychotherapist and a skilled pastoral counselor combine their special talents and insight to describe the process of individual caregiving.

Dudley, Carl S. *Making the Small Church Effective.* Nashville: Abingdon, 1978.
The author makes a compelling case for the place of a small church in our society.

Dudley, Carl S. "Membership Growth, The Impossible Necessity." *Christian Ministry,* Vol. 8, No. 4, July, 1977.

Feucht, Oscar E. *Everyone a Minister.* Philadelphia: Westminster Press, 1974.
This book is a guide to churchmanship for laity and clergy. It sets forth in practical terms the startling possibility of a biblically-inspired priesthood of believers.

Galloway, Dale E., *20-20 Vision—How to Create a Successful Church.* Portland, Ore.: Scott Publishing Co., 1986.
A master plan for growth with the model of hundreds of Tender Loving Care groups meeting during the week throughout the metropolitan area of Portland where "Heart-to-Heart" fellowship takes place.

Getz, Gene A. *Sharpening the Focus of the Church.* Chicago: Moody Press, 1974.
The author discusses why the church exists, how to build the church through New Testament principles, administration, and organization.

Goppelt, Leonard. *Apostolic Times.* Translated by Robert A. Gueloch. London: Adam & Charles Black, 1970.
Fine scholarship recounts the development of the church and her message in the first century.

Griffiths, Michael. *God's Forgetful Pilgrims.* Grand Rapids: Wm. B. Eerdman's Publishing Co., 1979.
This excellent biblical study emphasizes the church as a body and its need for growth and development corporately.

Hahn, Celia Allison, James R. Adams, Anne Gavin Amy. *My Struggle to Be a Caring Person.* Washington, D.C.: The Alban Institute Inc., 1981.
This leader's manual outlines ten training sessions for a support group in caring and sharing.

Haugk, Kenneth C. *Christian Caregiving—A Way of Life.* Minneapolis: Augsburg, 1984.
This book describes Christian caregiving and explains how the Christian can make it a way of life.

———— and William J. McKay. *Christian Caregiving—A Way of Life, Leader's Guide.* Minneapolis: Augsburg, 1986.
This complete leader's guide makes it easy to train church members in distinctively Christian caring skills.

Jefferson, Charles. *The Minister as Shepherd.* Manila: Living Books for All, 1973.
This is the most heartwarming book that I've read on shepherding and pastoral care. It reminds the reader of his responsibilities as one of God's shepherds to do a better job. It is a convicting book.

Keller, Phillip. *A Shepherd Looks at Psalm 23.* Grand Rapids: Zondervan Publishing House, 1970.
An excellent devotional book with remarkable insights on shepherding by an author who was a shepherd of sheep.

Kittel, G., and Friedrich, G., editors. *Theological Dictionary of the New Testament.* 9 Vols. Grand Rapids: Eerdmans, 1968.
A superb source for word study in the original language. The writers trace the development of a word under study from its classical period through its development in scriptural usage.

Kraemer, Hendrick. *A Theology of Laity.* Philadelphia: Westminster Press, 1958.
A very insightful overview of the history and theology of a lay person's role.

Lyra Jr., Synesio. *A New Laity.* Garden Grove, Calif.: Lay Minister's Training Center.
A handbook that focuses on the history and importance of the laity.

Miguens, Manuel. *Church Ministries in New Testament Times.* Westminster, Md.: Christian Classics, 1976.
A fine study of official order with the duties of offices in the Christian community in the New Testament and patristic periods.

Miller, Kenneth R. and Mary Elizabeth Wilson. *The Church That Cares.* Valley Forge, Pa.: Judson Press, 1985.
The authors present a practical step-by-step process for gearing a church to action in beginning a caring ministry.

Neighbor Jr., Ralph W. *Shepherd's Handbook.* Houston: Touch Outreach Publications, 1986.
A handbook on shepherding. It has excellent ice-breakers and practical ideas for share groups.

Nelson, Carl and Martha. *The Ministering Couple.* Nashville: Broadman Press, 1983.
Features couples and ministry. The emphasis is on lay couples modeling the Christian marriage and ministering effectively in the local church.

Oswald, Ray. "Pastor's Passages," *Leadership*, Vol. IV, No. 4, Fall, 1983.

Perry, Lloyd. *Getting the Church on Target.* Chicago: Moody Press, 1977.

The author outlines ways in which the local church can be revitalized. Chapter four deals with developing a church's organizational structure. It is a well-balanced book with excellent help in the "how tos" of leadership.

Quiet Time. Downers Grove: Intervarsity Press, 1977.

Schweizer, Edward. *Church Order in the New Testament.* Naperville, Ill.: Alec R. Allenson, 1961.

This book provides excellent materials for the various stages of development in the first-century church. It presents a strong case for the great diversity and variety of New Testament churches.

Scipion, George. *Timothy, Titus, and You.* Phillipsburg, N.H.: Pilgrim Publishing Co., 1975.

This is an excellent manual designed to train elders (or potential elders). It takes elders through all the potential passages pertaining to their qualifications and ministry. Each lesson has a homework assignment.

Shedd, Charles W. *The Pastoral Ministry of Church Officers.* Atlanta: John Knox Press, 1974.

Sider, Ronald J. *Rich Christians in an Age of Hunger.* Downers Grove, Ill.: InterVarsity Press, 1977.

Stedman, Ray C. *Body Life.* Glendale, Calif.: Regal Books, 1972.

The author makes an excellent case for a participatory fellowship that embodies New Testament *koinonia.* It is a "how to" book on church relationships.

Stevens, R. Paul. *Liberating the Laity: Equipping All the Saints for Ministry.* Downers Grove, Ill.: InterVarsity Press, 1985.

This book, exploring new options for pastors, tentmakers, and lay people, provides structure and strategies to best equip all the saints for ministry.

Stowe, Eugene L. *The Ministry of Shepherding.* Kansas City, Mo.: Beacon Hill Press, 1976.

This book is a study on pastoral care from the senior pastor's perspective.

Thomas, Donald F. *The Deacon in a Changing Church.* Valley Forge, Penna.: Judson Press, 1969.

The book is written to give assistance to lay leadership in a world of change. The beginning dealing with biblical principles for the ministry of the diaconate is insightful.

Thompson, Bernard. *Good Samaritan Faith.* Ventura. Calif.: Regal Books, 1984.

Outlines a strategy for meeting the needs of a lay person's friends and neighbors. It outlines a step-by-step plan for organizing local church-board caring ministries.

Tillapaugh, Frank R. *The Church Unleashed: Getting God's People Out Where the Needs Are.* Glendale, Calif.: Regal Books, 1982.
The author in a model under his own leadership proves the validity of unleashing church people for ministry in the world and utilizing the gifts the Holy Spirit gives them.

Treadway, Charles F. *The Deacon Family Ministry Plan Resource Book.* Nashville: Convention Press, 1979.
A fine basic handbook for deacons to use to facilitate their watch-care ministry.

von Campenhausen, Hans. *Ecclesiastical Authority and Spiritual Power.* Stanford, Calif.: Stanford University Press, 1969.
The author does a scholarly work of developing the offices of the church and their authority into the patristic period. The book is of extreme importance in understanding the power structure of the early church.

Unpublished Material

Bailey, David D. "Manual for Lay Ministers of Pastoral Care." Paper used in the training program of the Garden Grove Community Church of Garden Grove, Calif. (Mimeographed.)
Contains the overview of the entire lay ministry program of the Garden Grove Community Church, its training materials, and sample correspondence.

Bixby, Howard. "Deacon Caring Kit." Material used by Calvary Baptist Church. Grand Rapids, 1979. (Tapes)
Six cassette tapes explain the Deacon Caring Ministry of Calvary Baptist Church of Grand Rapids, Michigan. The material is helpful in the practical "how to" of developing a deacon ministry.

Board of Education of the UPCUSA. "The Ministry of the Deacons in the UPCUSA Today." Philadelphia, 1963.
A collection of seven unpublished manuscripts presented at a consultation held July 15–19, 1964, prior to the report on "The Nature of the Ministry" made to the 176th General Assembly of the United Presbyterian Churches in the United States of America. The recommendation was made that the lay office of deacon be abolished in favor of using that title to designate a form of clerical ministry. The manuscripts provide a wealth of material on many different aspects of the diaconate. Titles include: "Lay Ordination in the New Testament Context"; "The Problem of the Diaconate"; "Lay Ordi-

nation and the Diaconate"; "The Diaconate in the Reformed Tradition"; "An Interpretation of the Diaconate in the Light of Pre-Reformation Church History"; and "The Role of the Diaconate in the Contemporary Church."

Ver Straten, Charles. "Changing Baptist Deacons into Lay Shepherds." Denver: Conservative Baptist Theological Seminary, 1980. (Doctoral dissertation.)
This is the documentation of the project which gave birth to this book.